BEFORE YOU DATE HIM, INVESTIGATE HIM

Finding the truth about online suitors, cheaters and scammers while protecting yourself and learning how to be your own online investigator

Sam Del Rosario and Louis A. Savelli

ISBN 13: 9780615686950
ISBN 10: 0615686958

Published by Homefront Publishing, 4809 Avenue N, Suite 180, Brooklyn, New York 11234

Toll Free: (877) 232-7500 Fax: (718) 209-4646

All photos appearing at the beginning of each chapter, and the cover photo, have been purchased and licensed through Dreamstime Inc.; **http://www.dreamstime.com/**

For Our Families

The Del Rosario family

The Savelli family

Thanks for your support and putting up with so many phone calls, much lost family time and our many late nights on the computer to get this book done.

Contents

Devil's Advocate
(Our Version of a Disclaimer or Warning)

While the online dating scene, today, is far more advanced and mainstream than ever, it can still lend itself to deceptions, scammers and serial killers. Regardless, the purpose of this book is not to frighten you into seclusion and lock your computer in a dark hall closet never to be opened again. The purpose is to make you aware of the potential dangers and 'less than truthful' people that may be lurking on the Internet and among the Online Dating scene. Here, occasionally, we are going to be the devil's advocate or the voice of reason and your big brother warning you and exposing the bad people who don't have your best interest in mind.

Our intention is to make you more aware, not scared. Our intent is to expose that small portion of Internet users who have malicious intentions and arm you with awareness, more options and the ability to investigate anyone you meet online. In other words, we are going to help you identify the truth behind the emails, texts, chats, Facebook pages and dating profiles.

We will provide you with the information, resources, and examples and help you develop the skills to find out the real deal. At the end of this book, you will be able to do it all on your own. Go ahead... check out that guy who has been sending messages to your online dating account or that cute guy you've been flirting with! Is he married? Does he have kids? How many dating profiles does he have? And what about your current boyfriend or husband...is he cheating with some online home-wrecker? You will even be able to check it out on your own, using the Internet. You will also be able to find out what people are saying about you and what people are reading about you! You will easily become your own Internet Detective!

The Authors

Sam Del Rosario and Lou Savelli met five years ago during an investigation that involved terrorist activity related to New York and Pennsylvania. Sam was a detective in the Allentown, PA area and Lou was the detective supervisor of NYPD's Terrorist Interdiction Unit. Not only did Sam and Lou become colleagues in this highly critical investigation but they became fast friends.

Both born and raised in New York City, Sam grew up in the Bronx while Lou grew up in Brooklyn. They had a lot more in common, too. They had both made it their life's quest to aggressively hunt down criminals and both had always worked so hard that they were looked at as zealots and idealists. While Sam had also become a well-respected trainer within his region, Lou was one of the nation's leading trainers and police writers. The two criminal investigators joined forces to train law enforcement officers in the US and overseas and now to bring this book, and its investigative techniques, to life.

Sam Del Rosario

Sam Del Rosario is now a police officer in the City of Bethlehem, PA and a Deputy Coroner for the Lehigh County Coroner's Office. He is one of the leading innovators on Internet Investigations and Gathering Intelligence through Social Networking Sites. He has conducted countless successful criminal investigations and has utilized his skills with Internet resources and computers to enhance and solve many of these investigations. Sam is part of Homefront Protective Group's Criminal Investigation Training Team providing training to law enforcement officers across the world. Sam has earned a Master's of Arts degree in Criminal Justice, with an emphasis on investigative forensics, and a Bachelor's of Science degree in Criminal Justice. He is a graduate of the Federal Law Enforcement Training Center's Criminal Investigator Training Program, and has received extensive training on various topics to include forensics, criminal investigation, computer forensics, and internet investigations. Sam has provided training on internet investigations to various public safety agencies, private corporations and school districts. He can be reached at **sdelrosario@ homefrontprotect.com**.

Lou Savelli

Lou Savelli retired as a detective supervisor from the NYPD after 21 years of service. He is the author of several books and dozens of articles related to criminal investigations and has appeared on the History Channel, Fox News Channel and other television and print media. His investigations have been highlighted in Time Magazine, History Channel's Gangland Series and several periodicals. He is the President of Homefront Protective Group, the leading provider of law enforcement training programs and Homefront Security, a New York based Investigations and Security firm. He can be reached at **homefrontprotect@aol.com**.

Sam Del Rosario and Lou Savelli provide expert investigative assistance to police departments and private citizens, especially as it pertains to Internet and Computer crimes and the use of gathering information from Social Networking sites. They have helped and empowered countless victims take control of their lives through conducting their own investigations via the Internet. They have done so, again, and made it fun and easy, in this book.

Introduction

Though advertised statistics claim 1 out of every 5 relationships start online these days, we believe it is much higher. In fact, if you consider the cheaters, the liars, the sexual criminals and the scammers that are developing relationships for their own less than honorable reasons, you can easily double or triple that statistic. After having a lot of experience helping people, especially women who have fallen prey to online Romeos, who were really wolves in sheep's clothing and the criminal miscreants that troll the 'net seeking their next victim, we can only come to one conclusion. The amount of deception and ill-intentions in the online dating world, and the Internet in general, is frighteningly high.

As criminal investigators, long before the Internet age, it was our business and responsibility, to stay one step ahead of criminals. With wide retail availability of computers and the explosion of the Internet during the early nineties, we each jumped in with both feet and welcomed these new technological resources as an information tool as well as an investigative and crime-fighting tool. Almost immediately, we recognized the ease for which criminality would reach unsuspecting victims, especially those who were not tech savvy or somewhat naive. Also, almost immediately, victims started appearing at our doorsteps, though separate doorsteps, seeking help from online scammers and identity thieves. It was apparent that criminals and Internet monsters, like sexual predators, were far more adept at navigating and manipulating the Internet for their own sordid benefit than the current law enforcement capabilities could fight.

While over a decade past the terrorist attacks of September 11th, 2001, the amount and variety of crimes and heinous Internet victimization is far too commonplace. In fact, there is almost no user of the Internet that has not been victimized, at least as an attempt, by some predator, whether a sexual criminal or financial criminal. Now, the 'net as we know it today, is a predator's playground. The rest of us are only carefully stepping through its minefield hoping it doesn't capture our identities, our dignity and our innocence.

What we have done in this book is to provide our readers with self-protection and self-investigation techniques. They will be illustrated through the use of actual case studies from real victims coupled with step by step, easy to follow, procedures. Many of the victims mentioned in this book were our clients, friends and average citizens, who found themselves at the wrong end of the Internet. Some came to us from law enforcement channels and others through referrals from people we have helped in the past. Each was the victim of one or more of a variety of Internet predators. These predators ranged from identity thieves, con artists, sexual predator criminals, pornographers, child sexual predators to the most common which was online womanizers seeking to take advantage of an unsuspecting lady's loneliness, good nature or trusting soul. Our job was to find out the true intentions of the other person and to protect our friends, clients and citizens from further victimization. It seems, unfortunately, there is an overabundance of victims out there.

Why do we trust online acquaintances? Why do we, as a society, assume that written communication is also a sign of veracity? Is it that we have been trained through our lives to think, 'if it is written down it is the truth'? Is that from the old saying, "If it isn't documented, it never happened"? Who knows? What we do know, is people all over the world believe that if it is written in a book, or on the Internet, it is far more believable or valid than if it is when verbally stated. As we know, and hopefully others, that may not always be the way it is. Books, newspapers, magazines, television, and the Internet are laden with snake oil salesmen, 'spin' doctors, and a host of others seeking to profit, in some way, off the trusting nature of others.

Part of this phenomenon, in our combined opinion, is that people are basically lazy and don't want to do the painstaking research to get at the truth or bottom line. We are all like that. It is easier to accept what is written than to challenge it and find out the real deal. The Internet goes far beyond this phenomenon. When you look at something and conduct a simple search, you can find many similar Internet sites that claim the same thing. Therefore, it must be true! And what about that guy you met on the popular dating site? You know, the site that claims to carefully screen their members. And that guy seemed great! He said he's single. He likes long walks on the beach. His picture is hot! It must be true! **MAYBE NOT!**

Well, here lies the real truth, or at least a way at getting at the truth. This book, us and you, only have one goal in mind. That goal is to protect you and get at the truth, whatever it is. We have no connection to any dating site, Internet mogul or online ladies man. We are committed to you and our integrity. Let's venture, together, on this journey to find out the truth by exposing Internet fraudsters and show you how easy it is to do this yourself. Let's go!

Chapter 1

Looking for Love in Online Places:
Is he really as good as he sounds?

Did you ever meet someone on the street, in a restaurant, or some other social situation and later that evening you find a "friend request" in the inbox of your Facebook account? If you're being honest with yourself, you are probably shaking your head "yes" right now. What are your first thoughts after you get such a bold request? Is this guy for real? Is he a stalker? Or worse... the Craigslist Killer! But wait! You say his profile says that he is tall, athletic, loves puppies, his favorite movie is 'Chocolat' with Johnny Depp and he loves long walks on the beach. If you believe such a man exists then you have already accepted the friend request and can skip to the next chapter because at this point we can't save you. Ok, yes we can! However, if you are cynical like us then you know that this guy seems too good to be true, and you are probably right.

Unfortunately, too many people fall prey to the danger of online dating, and amazing profile pages touting to be Mr. Right when actually, he is Mr. Wrong or worse he is going to steal your money, or worse! Case in point, we once investigated a case where a single, middle-aged woman with children, received a wonderful comment on her MySpace account, which reads as follows:

> *"Hello beautiful,*
>
> *I was searching through MySpace and came across your profile and I was stunned by your beauty. I noticed that you like walking on the beach and watching chick flicks* (A good liar will have already scouted your profile). *I too love chick flicks and walking on the beach. I also see that you are single, and have a child. I love children. I was wondering if you were interested in chatting with me. About me, well... I am a single father and I own my own company. I travel the world a lot, which makes it difficult to meet the right woman. I was hoping maybe WE could one day travel the world, and live a lovely life as a family. Please write me back.*
>
> *Love,*
>
> *Cassanova"* (or Paul, we could never remember his name).

The above case is a perfect example of what we call in the law enforcement and private security business "Social Engineering," and unfortunately, our client fell for it. To make a long story short, our client eventually was conned into providing *"Cassanova"* with her bank account information, a $2500 loan, and shipping numerous electronic and computer parts to Nigeria. It was later learned that the items were purchased with stolen credit cards obtained from the Internet. Additionally, because of her involvement, she was listed as a suspect in this fraud ring, but was eventually cleared of any wrongdoing (by us), and obviously highly embarrassed. Unfortunately, this story is just one of many in the United States and across the Globe, and highlights a significant and growing problem.

The Internet has a plethora of information on almost everyone and everything, and much of this information is readily available to you. Oftentimes, we find ourselves perusing profiles of people who we have just met or are interested in based on the information they provide in their profile. However, can you trust that the information they are providing is truly who they are. Or are they providing you with information about who they are posing to be?

Online Dating Statistics

According to a study conducted by the Pew Internet and American Life Project entitled "Online Dating", approximately 10 million people have admitted that they were actively looking for a romantic relationship via the Internet. This number is only increasing, and many of the social settings we have grown up in such as a bar, clubs, and other settings have been replaced with Internet chat rooms, Internet hangouts (Google+ feature) and virtual meeting places. In the same study, cited above, approximately 66% of Internet users surveyed agreed that online dating is dangerous and poses some risk because of the amount of information that becomes available in an online dating environment. Many individuals do not understand that information is power, and once you expose this information you relinquish some of your own power and become vulnerable to online exploitation. Yet millions of individuals searching for love continue to post their personal information online, and share that information with individuals they only know by an avatar or screen name.

The business of dating, specifically online dating, is big business in the United States and across the world. It is estimated that the dating service industry pulls in about $2.1 billion dollars a year in the US alone with approximately 53% of these earnings going towards the online dating scene. There are hundreds of dating sites out there with millions of profiles of "single" individuals looking for love. Some websites specifically target married, or what we like to call the "monogamy challenged", individuals who are looking for discreet fun. Websites such as

Adultfriendfinder.com, F$&kbook.com, and Ashleymadison.com are sites geared towards individuals who are looking for that extra thrill in their life, which undoubtedly include infidelity. Then there are the prowlers, stalkers, and creeps who are trolling the Internet for vulnerable women who they can target for various reasons.

I only have one side, my good one

Many individuals who establish online dating and social networking accounts have several factors they should consider. Some of these considerations can range anywhere from the amount of information they will publicly post to the photograph that best represents who they are as a 'profile picture'. The Internet can be brutal, and it is not for the faint at heart. If you look like Shrek then chances are your comment box will be empty with the exception of a few comments from some random guys stating, *"Dude, you ugly!"* or some other insensitive comment. Let's be honest, how many profile pictures have you posted that you would consider them some of your most unflattering photos? Of course, you try to post your 'best', most photogenic, portraits. When someone establishes an online account, they typically want to present the "best" of what they have to offer. However, when does presenting your 'best' photo become outright lying about who you are?

An example of the 'profile picture' hoax came to us in the form of an investigation we had conducted involving a harassment/stalker case. In this case, the victim met her online lover in an Internet chat room labelled, *"Looking for Romance".* She received a private message from our Internet "Casanova" who requested a 'private chat' with her. That should have been her first indication that something was wrong. Her unidentified lover began his conversation with her by using information she had previously volunteered. He used information about who she was, where she was from, and then the discussion evolved into relationships, etc... Of course, he described himself as the ideal mate. He said he was tall, dark and handsome of course. The conversation continued for quite some time until it was graciously ended.

Later that evening, our unsuspecting victim received a friend request on Facebook from a guy who claims to be the same male who had conversed with her earlier that evening. A photo of a very attractive male who matched the "tall, dark, and handsome" description she received earlier was accompanying the message.

Our victim had continued her online relationship with this alleged handsome fellow for several months until one day while perusing a shopping catalog she recognized a familiar face. It so happens that our "tall, dark, and handsome" is, in fact, a male model in a local JC Penny catalog. Now, there were two things running through our victim's mind. The first thought would be that she was the luckiest woman in the world, and Mr. Right was a gorgeous model who was interested in her. The second thought is this guy, who she has shared her inner most thoughts and feelings, is not who he says he is. Our victim rightfully confronted the phony model with this evidence, and of course, he presented her with a million excuses. She eventually discontinued her online relationship with the online "Casanova," but unfortunately, that was only the beginning. For the next several months, 'lover boy' (Casanova) decided he wanted to continue to contact the victim, and repeatedly e-mails, posts, and even obtains the victim's phone number through the Internet. Casanova continued to contact the victim and his messages escalated from appeals to the victim to continue their relationship to all out threats and verbal abuse. The victim eventually decided that she has had enough, and contacted our agency. Fortunately, based on information obtained from the victim, we were able to identify the online Casanova and put a stop to his stalker behavior.

Cases such as the one described above are not unusual, and I am sure you or someone you know has fallen victim to the profile picture hoax. If fact, some of you may have posted a picture of yourself that is, maybe, a little different than the way you look now. When the person is outright lying about who he is, there is reason to be concerned.

Looking for Mr. Right in the wrong place

As we had briefly mentioned earlier, online dating is a huge market, and there are literally hundreds of sites claiming to be the best chance at finding love. Some of these sites even claim to have a special procedure to weed out individuals who are married or who are not compatible with your profile. However, there have been several instances of the online Casanova making his way into these trusted sites, and successfully manipulating his 'marks' (victims). So, how do you know the site you are dealing with is the 'real deal'? Your first clue should begin at the Home Page of the site. What do you see? Does it appear that the site is well organized, and professional? Does the site appear unprofessional and have sexual innuendos throughout? Some individuals meet people online through Social Networking sites like Facebook, MySpace, Xanga, Bebo, and others where your information may be publicly available for all to see. These types of details are important when you decide to go out on the Internet to look for your Mr. Right.

When selecting an online dating site you must research the reputation of the site, and the success of the site concerning your ultimate goal: Finding Mr. Right! Throughout the book, we will show you various techniques to research information about a website, a person, and that crazy neighbor who lives down the block from you. We all have one, or more. Some of these skills you will also be able to apply to your work life as well. However, at this stage of the game the first step in protecting yourself from the dangers of the Internet is choosing the right website, and knowing when to be suspicious of it.

Chapter 2

When in doubt, check him out: *Check him out ANYWAY!*

How can you have doubt about someone you met online? I mean, you have seen his profile and his picture. I'll bet you have even chatted with him. You are practically old friends. C'mon, this is the Internet age. People fall in love everyday with someone they met online that they have never physically met. What do you have to worry about? Just meet him. What do you think? Is he going to be an axe murderer or something worse – UGLY? Of course you should CHECK HIM OUT, when there is doubt. You should check him out anyway, just to be safe!

Even though this is the Internet age, people can hide their true intentions and their true identity. It happens all the time. For those of us who dated before the Internet age made online hook-ups a household word, we actually met face to face or were introduced by friends, co-workers or relatives. That was always an experience but it was a lot safer. Some people even met in bars and nightclubs – YIKES! Meeting someone online, though convenient, is still a risky thing, as detailed in the previous chapter discussing that online Casanova. You should always want to know something more about an online acquaintance you are intending to meet, even more than you currently know, especially since online data can be slightly, grossly or criminally, misleading.

"When in doubt, check him" out is good solid advice. It's our advice! When your gut instincts tell you something is fishy, it's time to get your pole! And ask yourself, *"How many times has your gut been wrong?"* Your gut, common sense, and a little bit of Internet detective work, can save you lots of heartache in the future. It may even save your life!

To better understand this advice, and learn a quick tip on Internet detective work, here is a recent case we worked.

Alyssa was a shy, 22-year-old woman. She was far from the cheerleader type but she was attractive and had a great smile. Her long, dark hair and striking features made her very photogenic. She came from an old-fashioned family, had old-fashioned values and old-fashioned ways about her. She has always had trouble meeting guys because of her shyness and friends prompted her to try meeting guys online. She was, at first, reluctant to jump into online dating but, with a little help from her friends, set out on one of the more well known, reliable, online dating sites. After her friends helped her set-up her dating profile and uploaded a great picture of her, Alyssa was well on her way to meeting Mr. Right. Within a day, Alyssa had more male suitors, than she had in her entire life. She was a bit apprehensive, but it was exciting. After a long stressful day at work, Alyssa came home, threw off her shoes and sat in front of her desktop. As soon as she logged into her dating account, she saw the red flags popping into her 'in box', literally! She had seven guys wanting to get to know her better. Two wrote *'Let's hook up!"* Another wrote,

"Your dream date wants to chat!" In addition, the next four were a bit more subtle and merely wrote, *"I want to get to know you better!"*

Alyssa, being shy, was immediately reluctant to even open the messages from the three more aggressive suitors but carefully went through each of the others who wanted to get to know her better. She thought it was fun and it made her feel more desirable than she has ever felt before. One of the online male daters really caught her attention. This guy was like something out a 'chick flick'. His first email immediately set him aside from the rest. Alyssa was intrigued. She definitely wanted to get to know him better.

Here is his email:

> *FROM: OldFashionGuy*
> *TO: Alyssa570*
> *SUBJECT: I want to get to know you better!*
> *Hi Alyssa! How are you? I am new at this online dating thing. My friends pushed me into it. So, please bear with me. I am kind of shy and find it hard to talk about myself but here it goes, anyway.*
>
> *I am 24 years old. I live in eastern Pennsylvania and work in New York City. It's a long drive each morning but the electricity of NYC is something I really needed to get me out of my shell. I am a junior stockbroker in a large firm but I am going to work hard to own the company someday! LOL. I haven't dated much and the girls I meet at work are too fast for me. My parents instilled their old fashioned ways into me and I like to take things slow. I am not attracted to girls who wear a lot of make-up and eight inch heels. Even though I am six feet tall, I am afraid they may break an ankle and I won't have the proper medical training to fix it.*
>
> *I am not looking for lots of dates because I prefer monogamy. I am looking for someone who has the same family values, dreams and respect for people that I have. I would LOVE to meet a girl who is a little bit shy and we can explore the excitement of the big city together because it's more fun when you*

have someone to share it with. I like Broadway plays, Central Park and quiet dinners on the upper Eastside. But I don't have anyone to share those things with because of my shyness.

Well, enough about me! If it is not too forward, I would really love to get to know you better. Tell me about your thoughts, your likes, your dislikes and your dreams. What lies behind that pretty face in the profile? Looking forward to hearing from you! ...OldFashionGuy

Alyssa liked this guy right of the bat. She took a look at his profile and saw his photo. "He was hot..." she thought to herself. And he didn't look like a shy old fashioned guy but she never gave it a second thought. Alyssa quickly answered his email and told him lots of things about herself. It was as if she couldn't wait to spill her thoughts to this old fashioned guy, as luck would have it, from Pennsylvania who was intrigued by the electricity of New York City, just like her.

Alyssa read the emails from the other guys but kept coming back to OFG (OldFashionGuy). They emailed back and forth, and except for him calling her Alice in one of his emails, he seemed consistent, sincere and a good catch. He explained the Alice mistake like this: "I guess I should apologize for calling you Alice but I can't. My mother's name is Alice and you remind me so much of her. I told her all about you. I told her how nice you are and so very pretty. I really respect my mom's opinion. She's old fashioned and a great judge of character. My mom said she thinks you sound like someone really special and I agree with her. She said we should meet in person but I didn't want to rush anything. TTFN, Alice, I mean Alyssa, I mean you know what I mean. LOL! It's like that old song: I want a girl, just like the girl that married dear old dad! Talk to you soon!!!!!!!!"

Alyssa read the email and couldn't wait to set up a face to face meeting with OFG. "He was perfect!" she thought. "An old fashioned guy who cares deeply about his mom and is looking for someone he respects just like his mom. That someone could be me!"

Alyssa was so excited she told all her friends. They were ecstatic for her. Alyssa read all the all emails from OFG to her few closest friends. Everyone was in agreement that she should meet this OFG and go on a date. Everyone, that is, but Mary. Mary had some bad experiences with online dating. Even though she met her fiancé online, she was slightly apprehensive for Alyssa. She felt it was definitely time for a face to face meeting but there were a few things she felt Alyssa should do first. She told Alyssa to talk to her fiancé's friend Jimmy. Jimmy was a state trooper in Pennsylvania who had a colleague with lots of experience in online investigations. Alyssa felt she was being disloyal to OFG if she had someone check him out but she said she would think about it. After reading over every email she received from OFG, Alyssa started thinking about something someone told her about the Internet, Internet dating and online surfing in general. It was *"if it's too good to be true, it is too good to be true!"*

Alyssa agreed to talk to Jimmy, the state trooper, who referred her to us. We immediately made Alyssa feel comfortable and didn't want her to feel embarrassed in any way nor to be concerned about OFG finding out. We did a few simple online searches on screen names with the name OldFashionGuy and added several endings from the most popular Internet Service Providers (ISP) and Social Networking Sites (SNS). Within our first few searches, we found OFG and we found his picture. It was the same picture he used on his dating profile and the same picture he used on several other dating profiles. In fact, we found him on over a dozen dating sites and a few with less than moral themes. With a few more searches we determined that the photo was definitely him, OFG. The only problem that arose is the OFG on the dating sites and in the photo showed a wife and two kids. He lived in PA and worked in NYC. And he wasn't 24 years old, he was 38. The photo had digital data that we uncovered showing it was taken by an old digital camera several years prior. We could only imagine what he looks like now. With only a few more strokes of the keyboard, we found out more about OFG. He really was an OFG. He was an Older Fat Guy than he was portraying himself and he had a receding hairline that would make Saint Anthony proud. His most current picture was on MySpace showing him and his beer belly playing ball with his

16 year old son while his wife and 14 year old daughter sat at a nearby picnic table with other people. The caption at the bottom of the photo saved us the trouble of checking the electronic data of that photo. It read, *'family picnic 2011, Mt Pocono'*.

We immediately called Alyssa and explained to her what we found. She asked if we could email her our findings and we agreed, as long as she swore she would not venture on a harassment quest on OFG and his family. She swore to us that she would not harass him, or his family, and she wouldn't even answer any of his future emails to tell him what she knew. She was very grateful and obviously sad and embarrassed at the same time.

As we told Alyssa and many other people we have helped, there are plenty of honest people online seeking to make a connection with the right person. Don't let the OFGs and other scammers discourage you from making friends and finding romance. The only thing we recommend is when in doubt, check him out, and as a good practice, check him out anyway!

Chapter 3

Past behavior is a good predictor of future behavior!

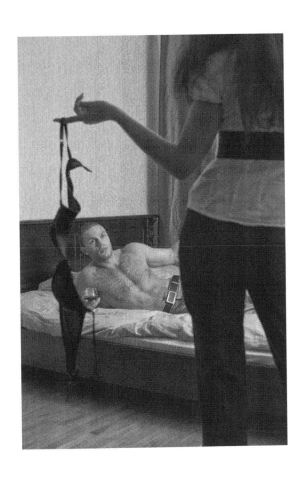

Nowadays, you can find just about any kind of information on the Internet. Everything from family photos to pictures of congressional wieners. Just ask a certain congressional representative from New York. The Weener! People are sharing so much information on the Internet that it is scary. For the skilled investigator or savvy news reporter the Internet is ripe with information that can be used to gather data such as addresses, telephone numbers, criminal histories, real estate records, civil records, and marriage licenses on a potential 'mark.' Are these individuals doing anything special? Not really! Most of the methods they use to research information on the Internet are readily available to the public, but many people are not aware that such information may exist or know where to begin their search for information That is where we come in (Drum roll please!). We will show you how to separate Mr. Right from Mr. Wrong by becoming your own investigator, and finding who the online 'Casanova' really is.

There are several online sites where you can obtain information about a prospective lover ranging from free government sources to fee based services through private data mining companies. The decision on which site is appropriate for you will depend on how bad you want information on your potential suitor, and whether you want an easy report that you can refer to. However, why spend all of your hard-earned money on some private investigator when you can have fun being your own detective, and get all of the answers yourself. More importantly, you are protecting yourself from some loser, con artist, or simply a jerk that is out to satisfy his own needs. There are many sources of information available to you that are completely free, and can answer the basic questions you might have. The key, as you will see, is how to find this information.

The first question most people should ask about someone they meet online is whether this guy has a history of harassing or stalking behavior. One method of finding this information out is by checking with you local Clerk of Courts where all criminal and civil filings are made in most states, and searching through a bunch of files. I know what you are thinking! This seems like a lot of work because IT IS a lot of work. But fear not, you will find that most states now have electronic court records that can be easily searched at the click of a button. Most states now comply with what is called the "Freedom of Information Act" (FOIA), "Freedom of Information Law" (FOIL), "Open Records" or similar laws, which are designed to provide the public with open access to government documents. These documents include criminal court cases, civil cases or judgments (think of divorce and law suits), and domestic related cases (think restraining orders and child welfare cases). Depending on what state you live in, you will have a vast network of databases that are at your disposal and can assist you in your search about Mr. Right.

For example, in Pennsylvania, New York, Illinois, Florida, California and other states you can lookup records on anyone who has been arrested for traffic violations, criminal violations, and more, by searching through each state's electronic court docket system. The keywords you should be searching for are "Dockets" or "Court records". Even if the case had been dismissed or the person was found "Not Guilty", you can still see those records. If you wanted to look someone up you would simply need his name, date of birth (if available, but not always necessary), and the county or town he lives in. That can be easily done with a Google or similar search by using the city or town he lives in as a keyword and the keyword "County". The search feature you would want would be the "participant" or "defendant" search, which will provide you with several text fields to fill out. If there is a record available you can open each document, and read the case summary. In some cases, you can even see whether the person had accepted a plea deal to include the criminal charges.

So why would this information be important, you ask? Well, what we have found is past behavior is a good predictor of future behavior. If our online 'Casanova' has several arrests for harassment, assault, or other violent behavior, what will stop him from being violent with you? There are just too many cases we have investigated in which our clients have been subjected to physical abuse from a man who has a solid history of domestic violence or just plain violence. That is not to say that someone with a criminal history cannot still be Mr. Right, but at least you can make sure that he is not absolutely Mr. Wrong. The amount of information available through courts is amazing and we will cover how to find out whether Casanova is married by using this same information later. With this little bit of information you will be able to discern if this guy is the real deal or full of boloney (Yes, it's bologna but we like to use baloney!) And there's another word for this, but we will play nice, for now.

Within this same system, you can also search for civil filings or cases against individuals for anything from Landlord/Tenant disputes to child support payments. This information may be important in determining whether your Casanova may have financial problems, and might be attempting to use you as a human ATM. Another use would be to see if his 'Baby Momma' is suing him for child support. There is a good possibility that you will not only find out through the defendant's (Casanova's) name, but you may even find out who the plaintiff (the suing party) is, which may turn out to be the other woman. We can give you story after story about 'Baby Momma drama', so think hard about whether you want to get in the middle of that mess. Whether it is financial problems or domestic, you are bound to find something through the court system. In Chapter 8, you will find instructions that show you how to locate court records and identify where, online, you can get them.

Another system that has great value is 'Inmate Databases' or 'State Corrections' records. Let's say you encounter information from the court records you searched using the preceding mentioned techniques and learned that your online friend has been convicted of a serious crime. There is a way to search whether your online Casanova was a resident at one of those luxurious State, County, or Local correctional institutions. Several services you can subscribe to notify you when an inmate will be released, when he is released, and whether he was released with supervision (probation or parole). The reasons such inmate services are available are mainly due to the Federal Crime Victims Act, and most, if not all, States have followed suit with a similar legislation. The purpose, of course, is to protect victims, especially domestic violence victims, by keeping them informed of the status of an inmate who may have assaulted or otherwise violated the victim. This important system, unfortunately, is widely underreported, and many people (especially victims) do not know it exists.

The good news is this information is also online, and very easy to access. There is one such website called the Victim Information and Notification Everyday (VINE) link system (www.VINELINK.com), which is a service that allows crime victims to obtain timely and reliable information about criminal cases and the custody status of offenders 24 hours a day. Almost all of the States participate in this program with the exception of about three (South Dakota, Kansas, and Maine). The system allows you to look up an individual, set an e-mail alert that notifies you of his status change and when he is released. If you have ever been a victim of a crime or have experience with this system, I am sure you can attest to the benefits. However, if you did not know about these valuable resources then stick with us and we will show you what it can do.

Probably one of the most memorable uses of the VINE Link came in the form of a request by one of our (the author's) friends. For the sake of the story, we will identify her as Sally. Sally met a man at work who befriended her and they exchanged contact information in the form of an e-mail address and phone number. The relationship continued like any normal relationship. It included conversations via e-mail and text messaging. After a period of time, Sally noticed a pattern in her communication with her male companion which she thought was quite odd. She realized he never emailed or texted her after 7 pm each day. Sally suspected that her male friend might be married. She was, however, reluctant to confront him, fearful of his reaction, and ultimately, the truth.

Sally consulted us and we recommended she look him up online using one of the many tools found in this book. She found a criminal history on him and we suggested checking VINE Link to see whether he ever served time in jail or prison. In an unlikely turn of events, Sally learned that he, not only spent time in prison, but was currently on Prison Supervised Work Release. As it turns out, he was not communicating with her past 7 PM because he had to report back to his prison cell once he finished working his shift, which is something he had failed to mention in his conversations with her. Now this is not to say that he was not a good guy, and maybe he was a little embarrassed about his current predicament, which is why he omitted this from her, however, should she really begin a relationship on a lie? I wouldn't think so. The most important aspect here is the information available and you (and Sally) cannot have too much of it. The more information you have, the more empowered you will be.

Chapter 4

Wow! He has 75,000 Facebook friends: *He must be a catch!*

Facebook friends? What the heck does that mean? Are they real friends? Will they lend us money? Will they drive us home if we had too much to drink? Did we grow up together? Did we go to the same school? Are their friends our friends? I'm confused? And how can someone have 75,000 friends? Who has the time? Do we even want 75,000 friends? Well, any guy who has 75,000 friends must be a catch. Right?

Let's take a look at someone with so many Facebook friends that he could win the Democratic Primary in any state. For the purpose of this chapter, his name is Derek Allan Smith. Derek is a real person. Although Derek isn't his real name, we'll call him that. We worked an investigation on Derek at the request of two highly embarrassed clients. Derek, to state it mildly, is an Internet-savvy criminal and a social networking con artist. He fooled a lot of people.

Derek is a modern social networking animal. If you look at his Facebook page, he is also a party animal. He has pictures of himself drinking at nightclubs with his friends, partying on the beach and skiing on the slopes of Sun Valley. What a guy? He's so exciting, so much fun, and he has 75,000 friends. Well, not that many, but a lot! He must be terrific.

He must be a great guy to have so many friends. Don't you want to be one of his friends - or do we? Derek used Facebook, Twitter and any other social media so he could manipulate them to bolster his background. He also used it to meet women and victims alike. In fact, the lines are seriously blurred here. So many women became his victim. Some almost married him. Some did!

Derek has been a con artist his whole life. He is a career criminal. Derek scammed a lovely young girl into marrying him, others into falling in love with him, several to become engaged to him, business people to give him money or some other benefit that he could morph into scamming someone else. He was a master at it. And the Internet offered a way to take his 'conning' globally. And he did! Derek has conned victims across his home country of Canada, his new home of the United States and several other countries where he chose to find people who believe that someone with so many Facebook friends has to be a good guy. Besides, all these people can't possibly be wrong.

Derek was a master at creating websites, linking himself to well-respected companies and even getting good 'straight' (honest) employment which he used to reinforce his business associations and resume. His use of these websites and social links were used, for a lack of a more accurate word, conning people. Derek knew people and they would vouch for him. Many were willing to place their names and reputations next to his because of his social (media) status and obvious connections. His connections were right there in black and white and red and any other color on the Internet. Well, if it's on the 'net, it must be true, right? That's what people say!

Derek met his last victims - at least for now. One was his fiancé, a 23 year old attractive Manhattanite who grew up in a wealthy family on the Upper Eastside. She fell for Derek's prowess with words and romantic manipulation through his emails and small gifts. After two months of online romancing, Derek came to Manhattan on a visit to find a job. He had a few job interviews lined up in his two-week visit. During that time, he spent every night and some days with MaryBeth. She was head over heels. At the end of the two weeks, Derek moved in with her.

And then there was Jonathan, who was a small record producer in New York City that has solid connections and an even more solid reputation. His name, which is obviously a pseudonym we created, is Jonathan Stanley. Jonathan owned and operated his small record company by himself and opened it with royalties from a hit song he wrote for a well known recording artist who will remain nameless. Jonathan is a good guy all around. He is honest, very well respected and a hard working music producer who was able to avoid the seedy side of the record industry until he met Derek.

Derek met Jonathan through mutual contacts in the Canadian music industry who recommended Derek as an up and comer who was moving to New York City to marry the girl of his dreams, a Manhattan Socialite, whom he met online. To Jonathan, not only was Derek and his connections a valuable find for his company but the romance story between Derek and his love is the stuff that 'hit' love songs are made of. Derek's contacts in Canada's growing hip hop industry told Jonathan about their business associate and his visionary ability to help music producers make the right international contacts. What Jonathan didn't know was that Derek's mutual hip hop moguls were also organized crime associates who had no problem recommending Derek to their business associates as long as they would benefit.

Jonathan hired Derek immediately. He felt that Derek and his alleged international contacts and visionary style would be the shot of adrenaline his company so desperately needed. Derek introduced MaryBeth, as his fiancé, to Jonathan. If you have been following closely, Derek introduced MaryBeth to Jonathan as his fiancé but that wasn't the truth at that time, or was it? MaryBeth thought it was cute and romantic since she was crazy about Derek. Derek knew it would help reel-in MaryBeth more than he had already done and Jonathan would like someone who was grounded and staying in New York rather than a Canadian who didn't have a permanent residence here.

Jonathan trusted his gut and asked Derek to start right away. Derek started working the next day. He brought in two new clients his first week (or did he?) and helped develop some key business associations for Jonathan's company. He was a welcome addition to the company, Jonathan thought. Within the first few months, Derek was a trusted employee taking on serious responsibilities and important business accounts. He had access to all the bank accounts, IT passwords, client lists and keys to the office. While he was able to bring in new business, he became exceedingly familiar with the company's old business clients. Jonathan even trusted him with his young children. You could even see them as the most recent friends on Derek's Facebook page. 75,003 Facebook friends and counting!

In only a few months, Derek was able to gain the trust of Jonathan, a smart businessman, while carefully and clandestinely using the company as another way to commit fraud and steal money. It even worked well impressing MaryBeth's wealthy parents who gave Derek and their daughter a large cash gift of $25,000.00 for their engagement. Derek was well on his way to a lucrative and happy future but it had nothing to do with staying at Jonathan's company or marrying his fiancé, MaryBeth.

One day, late in June, Derek called Jonathan to tell him that he would need the week off since his father was very sick. He had to return to Canada in a hurry. He gave Jonathan his parent's address and said that his cell phone would be on in case he or a client needed to contact him in an emergency. Derek told MaryBeth the same story and she insisted she go with him for moral support and to finally meet his parents. Derek said he would be back in a week and they would take a trip together in the near future, before the wedding, to meet his parents and his siblings, but now wasn't the right time. She was sad but agreed. That was the last time Jonathan and MaryBeth heard from Derek.

After a week of unreturned voice mail messages, both Jonathan and Derek's fiancé became extremely frightened that something bad had happened to Derek. Besides doing some investigating of their own, they got together and walked into the local precinct to ask for help. After speaking with a detective, Jonathan and Derek's fiancé became confused. The detective conducted a search of nationwide databases, international databases, criminal records checks, accident reports and other searches that is typical in a Missing Persons case, and gave them some unbelievable news. Derek Allan Smith, with the same date of birth, same Canadian SIN (Social Insurance Number) and same home address in Canada as their beloved Derek, died in 1999 at the age of 23 after a battle with Leukemia. The address coincided with the parent's address provided by Derek before he left. The detective sent Jonathan and MaryBeth home to get more information while he did some additional investigating.

Later that day, the detective, who we had previously worked with, called and told us the story. It was painfully obvious that the real Derek Allan Smith was a deceased person in Canada and the fake Derek, MaryBeth's fiancé and Jonathan's star employee, are two different people. Even the SIN that Derek was using, Canada's version of a Social Security Number, belonged to the deceased Derek Allan Smith. So far, it was only a case of identity theft, but what has Derek done to Jonathan's company and what has he stolen from MaryBeth besides her heart?

The detective asked us to work our magic on the Internet and see what we can find. By later that night, we found hundreds of traces of David Allan Smith on the Internet. There was so much inconsistent information and false data but it all led back to Derek, MaryBeth's fiancé. And that was definitely not his real name. As best we could determine, at this point, his name was David Sanford AKA James Sanford, Samuel David, David Golan, David Davis and a dozen other names with varying ages. (Yes, these are also names we just made up for this story so PLEASE don't call these people and threaten them!) He appeared on several websites, he was linked to several businesses, he had over 100 varied email addresses that we could find and extensively used Facebook, Twitter, MySpace, Xanga, Friendster, BeBo, and other social networking sites to maintain all of his identities and further his scams. In fact, there was at least one posting from one of his previous victims showing a photo of Derek accusing him of being a con artist and a fraud.

The next day the detective explained our findings to Jonathan and MaryBeth. He told them that Derek was a con artist and a thief and, most likely, had victimized each of them in more ways than the obvious. He urged them to take a close look at their personal and professional finances and to determine if any items of value were stolen. He warned that their identities were at risk of being used by someone like Derek. They were obviously upset. He also told them to determine if Derek stole from their close friends and business associates. Now, they became even more visibly upset. MaryBeth, who seemed to be in shock from the beginning, could not hold back her tears.

Two days later, the detective was again paid a visit from MaryBeth and Jonathan, as well as their attorney. They were visibly sad and told him they discovered money was missing from their bank accounts. MaryBeth, through her tears, informed that the $25,000.00 gift from her parents was missing from their joint bank account and other money from her personal accounts. Jonathan, also, told how he discovered his company checks were bounced to the tune of $80,000.00 so far. The detective immediately directed them to make formal criminal complaints against Derek and he would start an investigation and file for a warrant for his arrest.

The attorney, who accompanied MaryBeth and Jonathan, chimed in. He informed the detective that MaryBeth's family, because of their social and financial status, has chosen to avoid criminal complaints against Derek. He also said that Jonathan's business couldn't handle the negative publicity and Jonathan would not be filing formal criminal complaints at this time. As it turned out, he asked the detective for our contact information to retain us as private investigators and to help minimize the damage to MaryBeth's reputation and Jonathan's business.

Since the rest of the story is highly-confidential and we don't want ALL our secrets exposed, we will sum up what happened next. Within a few weeks, we located Derek in Arizona involved in another business and engaged to another girl, Sandra, he met online. We forwarded all the information we had found on him to several of his active, but varied, email accounts and gave him, among others, the following ultimatum:

"Move back to Canada, pay back MaryBeth all the money you stole from her, pay back Jonathan the money you stole from him, and break up with your current fiancé, Sandra (yes, we know about Sandra, you scumbag) and we will not forward all of our investigation results to the FBI, RCMP, OPP and several other police agencies in the US, Canada and Nova Scotia so you can spend the rest of your life in prison!"

MaryBeth and Jonathan got back most of the money from Derek. They were extremely appreciative. Derek broke up abruptly with Sandra. She didn't know why. Derek went back to Canada as fast as he could. Somehow, law enforcement found out about Derek and his criminal activities and he is currently wanted on serious felony charges in several countries. I wonder how the authorities found out?

Chapter 5

Rules of the Game

Like anything in life, before you embark on any new adventure you must know the rules. Similarly, playing a detective on the Internet requires that you learn some guidelines on how to find information and organize it in a sensible manner. Therefore, before we get into some of the specific components of searching the Internet, we want to provide you with a basic model on how to conduct your search and evaluate your results. Considering the topic of the book, you probably would not be surprised that we used the acronym C-A-T-C-H to explain our search model. The following breaks down what each letter means:

- **C**apture
- **A**ssess
- **T**est
- **C**ritique
- **H**old

First, **Capture** information from the Internet that you feel is relevant to your target, the person you want to investigate. In this case, your Mr. Right! Use information from multiple sources. The information can come from what he has told you, such as his name, address, phone number, and other information he has volunteered. You want to have as much information as possible so you can compare it against your sources of information. There can never be enough information at this point. The goal is to get as much information up front so there will be less to dig up later, of course, in a perfect world. Capture this information by making note of it by printing, screen capturing it, or e-mailing it to your In-box. Depending on the source of information available, you might be able to save it to your desktop or other location on your computer.

Next, you will want to **Assess** whether the information you have obtained on your target (Mr. Right) is reliable. For example, if you have obtained a criminal history from an official source such as the New York State Court System then you can be assume that the information is reliable. However, it is only as reliable as the government employee that entered the data. If your source of information comes from a blog site, personal web space, or other source with no real official backing, you might want to evaluate how you use this information. It may not be reliable. The Internet has a tremendous amount of information on it, but not all of it should be taken as credible or coming from a reliable source. The assessment phase will be an important part of your search as it will lead you into the next phase called Testing.

In the **Testing** phase, you will use the information you have obtained from the first two steps (Capture and Assess) and test the information on your target. This is not an all out confrontation, but a test of whether your target will be truthful about information for which you already know the answer. What you are doing at this point is evaluating the truthfulness of your prospective mate. This is no different from a customs official at the gate asking how you are doing today. You may think he or she is just bantering with you when in fact they are evaluating your behavior in response to their questions. You will learn that sometimes the simplest answer will reveal a lot about a person in context.

Once you have tested the information you have obtained on your target, the next step would be to critique whether the answers you have obtained have been truthful, deceptive, or you need more information. It is this step that you have to evaluate whether the responses given to you by your target are enough to satisfy your suspicions. You may find that some of the answers you have been provided may change the perspective of the information you had obtained from your first two steps. If that is the case, you can go back to the previous steps, and reevaluate the information from this new perspective. However, if you are not satisfied with the responses that you have received, it is time to go on to the next step, which is to hold them accountable.

The **Hold** phase is probably the most difficult one to deal with because it requires you make a decision. Holding someone accountable is often difficult especially when you may have feelings for this person, but it is unavoidable in a world of lies and deceit. We suggest you review the first few steps of the process to ensure you have the necessary information for your final decision. There are two ways you can handle this situation. First, you may not be that invested in the relationship, and you may prefer to just end it based on your findings. This is probably the easiest step, and may not require any further action on your part. If this individual is persistent he may want an explanation on why you stopped everything abruptly. It is up to you on whether you want to reveal your sources or cut your losses.

Finally, you can confront your target, with your findings and ask him to explain why he lied to you. Obviously, you should expect a response with the second situation and you may not like what you hear. Either way, the choice is yours on which approach you choose. In the end you will be making an informed choice, whether good or bad.

We cannot emphasize how important it is that you ensure you know whom you are dealing with before you become involved with them. Whether in business, love, family, or friends, knowing whom you are dealing with is important. Before we embark on our journey, we want to share with you the following case, which illustrates our point (although humorously).

The Honey Bun Bandit

It started like any other routine call; one of the authors was working patrol and was dispatched to a 911 call involving an intoxicated male inside a local gas station mini mart. The dispatcher reported the male was knocking food items off the shelf, and eating honey buns without paying for them. Arriving at the scene, with other police officers, there was this unruly, honey bun eating, fellow. He had been dressed as if he had just returned after a long night at a nightclub. He was a bit intoxicated (major understatement). He was sloshed!

We wondered how this handsome young man, who at this point was drooling with honey bun frosting on his face, arrived at the store. We looked in the parking lot and saw a lovely young woman who was waiting in a vehicle. She identified herself as his friend. She was obviously embarrassed by the whole thing. He tells us that they just stopped by the mini mart so he, her friend, can get something. We asked this young lady whether she would be willing to pay for the damaged items for her friend so we don't have to make this a theft case. She agreed and paid for the $20 in food product that her date had eaten or damaged. The guy was charged with public drunkenness.

Obviously, we were curious about how such a lovely lady would end up with this guy, and asked her whether this was her boyfriend. Again, with obvious embarrassment, she reiterated that they were friends. She stated this was their second date, and there would definitely not be a third date. As we laughed (being considerate of her feelings of course), she mentioned how she felt badly, and says "this isn't even the worst part." We asked her what she meant, and she told us that we would never believe how she met him. With our interest peaked, we asked her to explain, and she did. It appears this nice lady met, the "honey bun bandit" on a very popular online dating site, which shall remain nameless. Our next question to her was whether his profile stated that he loved honey buns so much. She laughed.

Unfortunately, there was more to this guy than we could tell her. We later learned that the "honey bun bandit" was no stranger to the police department, and had been arrested several times for various criminal offenses. One of those arrests involved domestic violence. Although we couldn't reveal the details of his criminal past, we made it clear in no uncertain terms that she should get rid of this guy. We were so clear that we even assisted her with deleting her own phone number from his phone, and escorted her back to the guy's home where she picked up her vehicle and drove home.

At the end of the day, we hope she had taken our advice and severed any ties with this guy. It is unfortunate that she is now listed in a police report as an "involved" person in a crime that she didn't have anything to do with. However, it is fortunate that she saw the guy for who he was before it was too late and before she had become too invested in the relationship. Could she have found out about this guy before their first date? Absolutely! That is the whole point of this book! Before you date him, investigate him. Now let's begin.

Chapter 6

Searching the Internet the Right Way

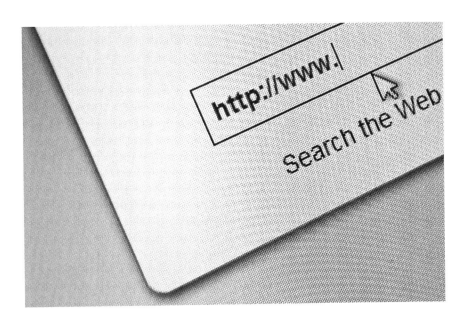

Many people use Internet search engines everyday without knowing why or how these search engines work. The first step in finding information on the Internet is to identify what tools are available to you, and how they work. With this understanding, we begin our discussion by explaining one of the most basic tools of the Internet, the Search Engine. We have all used search engines such as Google.com, Bing.com, Yahoo.com, Dogpile.com, AskJeeves.com, About.com, and many more. However, did you know that search engines only search a portion of the Internet? In fact, search engines only search a fraction of the entire web with Google topping the list as the site with the most 'indexed' pages. The truth is no singular search engine has all the information you may be looking for, which is why learning to search the Internet effectively is so important.

Search engines gather information from the Internet, and index it in a database usually by keywords or phrases. The search engines gather this information through the use of software called 'bots' (Robots) or 'Spiders' that crawl the Internet, hence the term 'web crawl', through active web links. The search engines file this information in their search engine database. If you are old enough to remember, this is similar to the card catalog file that was once in your local library. If you're not old enough to remember, forget we mentioned it, and thanks for making us feel ancient. As mentioned earlier the Internet is so large that only portions of it can be indexed at a time. Those areas that cannot be searched typically are password protected or behind a form of protection such as a firewall. (See the Glossary for the definition of firewall).

There are two types of Internet search engines available to the public. One is the 'Individual search' engine and the other is the 'Meta-search' engine. Rather than get any more technical, you just need to know that the individual search engines (such as Google, Bing, etc.) have their own databases and the Meta-Search engines do not have databases. The individual search engine will provide you with results that have specifically been indexed by that respective database. So, the larger the database, the more results you should see. Currently, Google has the largest database in the world, and touts itself as the best search engine out there. With Meta-Search engines, you are searching through multiple individual search engines, which are displayed for your review. However, sometimes the quality of the search is less than what you would get from an individual search engine.

We suggest you experiment with the various types of search engines out there to see which ones give you the most relevant results and are user friendly. It is up to you which search engines you use and why, but the key is understanding how they work so you can get the most information in the smallest amount of time. The next step is refining your search terms so you can narrow your results.

That is illogical, Captain!

Since we have briefly glanced over what a search engine is, which is a topic with thousands of books dedicated to it, our goal was to introduce you to some basic concepts so you can have a better understanding of how to locate information on the web. Now, we would like to show you a smarter method for searching the Internet for specific information. The skills we will show you are not only valuable for the purposes of this book, sifting through many Mr. Wrongs to find Mr. Right, but you will also find these skills useful in other areas of your life.

Several search techniques are used in a search engine database that can reduce the amount of irrelevant results you receive when you conduct a search. These techniques are fairly common to those in the research field, law enforcement, and librarians. In fact, your best source of information regarding the best methods to search for information is the library. There are many methods used in searching the Internet, but for our purposes we will only discuss two. The first method involves using the advanced features found in the database itself. Google, for example, has an advanced search field, which takes you to an input page and allows you to select from several options from a select menu of advanced features (See Figure 6.1).

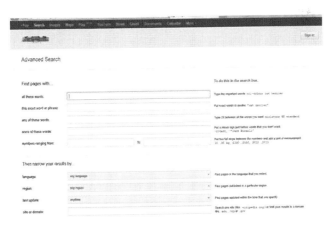

Figure 6.1 – Google Advanced Search Tool

Many other search engines also have advanced features that can be utilized in a similar manner. The second search method involves the use of specific 'modifiers' that tells the database what to include or exclude from a search result. The first of these 'modifiers' are called 'Boolean logic' operators, which are named after the 19th century logician, George Boole. Rather than get into the specifics of George Boole's role in creating these 'logical' equations, it is easier to say that the use of these equations have made a seemingly difficult task into a simple one by the mere insertion of the words "AND", "OR", "NOT" and "ADJ." (adjacent). These simple words can help you narrow down a search from millions of results to a few thousands if they are used properly.

An example, using the abovementioned search modifiers, can be demonstrated by using one of the most popular search engines, Google.com. If we were looking for a specific subject such as a place called "Bethlehem", we would simply insert the term into the search field on Google.com and the results at the time of this writing would number over 65 million. If you look through the first few pages of the results, you will see a mixed bag of information that you may find useful or irrelevant. The term "Bethlehem" can bring up results for a city in Pennsylvania, New York, or Israel. However, we are searching for specific information about Bethlehem, and we believe the location is Pennsylvania. We would insert the word "AND" between Bethlehem and Pennsylvania, which will now bring our results to about 26 million results. As you will see, by the addition of a simple word, we have reduced our results by 40 million, which is impressive, but still too much to go through (See Figure 6.2).

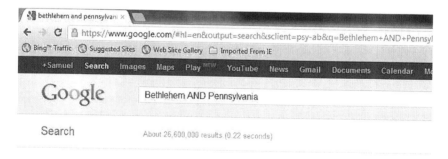

Figure 6.2 – Google Search with "AND" modifier

As we continue to add more specific terms, we begin to see a reduction in the number of search results we receive. Using the modifier "OR" will give us either of the two options we are searching for in our search parameters. The word "NOT" will eliminate the term we choose to omit from our results. For example, if we used the same search terms of "Bethlehem" and this time decided we did not want any results with "Pennsylvania" then we would insert the following equation: "Bethlehem" NOT "Pennsylvania." Overall, by using Boolean Logic you are able to reduce the number of irrelevant results you are looking for over time.

Another set of modifiers that are popular in search engines are mathematical operators such as the plus (+) and minus (-) signs. The plus (+) sign works in a similar manner as the "AND" modifier we previously discussed. If you wanted to find results for "Bethlehem" and "Pennsylvania" you will simply put a plus (+) sign between them like so:

Bethlehem + Pennsylvania = results

If you wanted to eliminate "Pennsylvania" from your search results, you would simply write the equation as "Bethlehem–Pennsylvania" which would eliminate any results that reference "Pennsylvania" (See Figure 6.3). By eliminating the term "Pennsylvania" you can narrow your search to a mere 232 million results (including the biblical birthplace of Jesus), which may or may not be what you're looking for. However, you can add several modifiers to your search terms, and eliminate even more results by mixing and matching each term to suit your needs.

Figure 6.3 – Mathematical Operator Search

So, you are probably thinking, "How does all this relate to investigating a potential date?" The answer is **everything**! Have you ever searched for yourself on the Internet? (Answer honestly!). Of course you have, we have all searched for our Google 'Doppelganger' online, and realized that we (you and us) are not the only ones with our names. When you do a search for a specific name, you will probably end up with a million or so different results, and most of them will key on specific portions of terms you have inputted in the search field. But, how do you find the person you are looking for? By now you should answer with, "by using Boolean Logic or Mathematical Operators?" Of course, we don't expect you to remember what they are called, but at least you will know how to use them.

For example, if we are going to search for a specific individual online, let's say "John Smith", we would do our homework first by obtaining as much information as possible about him. Recall the first step in our model in the previous chapter, which is to "Capture" as much information about your target. In this scenario, our mutual online friend "John Smith" will serve as the target of our suspicion. In your many conversations with "John" you learn from him that he is a car salesman from New York City. Okay, not the best job in the world, but it pays the bills. He claims to be one of the top sellers in his business, and was even recognized once for this achievement. John claims to be single, no kids, and lives somewhere in Manhattan. He has told you that he travels a lot and has family in New Jersey. John is a fascinating fellow and you would really like to meet him in person at some point. But wait, you have read this book and are now rightfully cautious about meeting someone online without investigating him. Shameful plug, we know! So how would you go about checking out the information provided by "John Smith" to make sure it is credible? Could something as simple as a mere Internet search be helpful? The answer is yes.

For the sake of this section, we will simply show you how to find information on "John Smith" by searching for him on one of the major Internet search engines. By no means are we showing a specific preference for one search engine over the other, but the most widely used search engine is Google, which is where we will start our search. Based on the paragraph above, we know that John is possibly a car salesman from New York, and he claims to live in Manhattan. We have a possible award that he was given for selling the most cars, and he claims he was recognized for it. "John" claims to have family in New Jersey, which may also be another source of information we can look for online. By recognizing the individual pieces of information we can put together in a search, we can begin to design a search pattern that we can use in our investigation.

Let us being with his name, "John Smith", we chose this name because, obviously, there will be a lot of them online. How many do you think live in New York State? At the time of this writing, there were 63 million results for "John Smith" on Google alone. If we added New York to our search (John Smith AND New York), we jump to 352 million, which is too much information. Now, I will add in Manhattan (John Smith AND New York AND Manhattan) and we are down to a mere 18 million. Now we are getting somewhere. You can begin to see how you can add more search terms to narrow your results down to what you want.

I now want to begin to associate "John Smith" with car sales, which is based on the information he had provided to us. I will perform the same type of search using his name, but this time I will search for car related terms. This is a perfect example where the "OR" logic term can be used. If we wanted to search for "Car Sales" you will get certain results, but aren't there other ways of saying "Car Sales?" You bet! "Auto Sales" would be another way of saying the same thing. So, when we build our search we want to include both "Car Sales" and "Auto Sales," which would look like:

"John Smith" AND "New York" AND "Car Sales" or "Auto Sales"

You will notice that your results include all terms related to our target, "John Smith," and "auto" or used "car" sales. The purpose here is to include any results that may be relevant to our target. In this case, there are multiple terms for car sales or auto sales so we want to include both in our search. If we wanted to search car salesman awards we can perform a similar search using those terms. Hopefully, you have asked what type of award he received such as the "Dealer of the Year" award from the National Automobile Dealer Association or some other similar award. If you didn't get it, don't worry! We will find it. You can search in the State where he works, and see if there is a similar association in it. In this case, there is a New York Automobile Dealer Association which you can check out to verify his story. A simple keyword search for "John Smith" will reveal whether he has ever been a recipient of an award or that he is full of baloney, bologna, or full of feces.

Finally, "John" referred to his family in New Jersey during one of your many conversations with him. Of course, we would suggest you ask him where in New Jersey, and if he was born there. If you have this information then you can search for the city or county where the family lives, and even check the local high school records. Using the same techniques we have just discussed, you will be able to obtain information about his family and any associations with him. In the end, you should be able to corroborate any information he may have given to you and you can assess whether this guy is for real.

If you are reading these pages and thinking *"Wow, isn't this a little creepy?"* You are probably right and we have not even scratched the surface, yet, about the types of information available to you. Some of you probably already begun a search on your boyfriends or significant other and are finding information that you may have not known about before. That is the beauty of the Internet, and information, in general. People do not realize how much of their lives are online and how easy it would be for someone to obtain this information. In the next chapter, we will discuss some of the types of information available, and how sometimes that information is forever memorialized on the net.

Chapter 7

Seek and Ye shall Find
... *and Trust Your Gut!*

It is amazing what you can see when you are looking for it and when you trust your gut. A little bit of awareness, and a lot of instincts, can lead to a lot of discovery. By no means are we telling you that everyone is out to get you nor that everyone is the Craigslist Killer! We just want you to look, listen and trust your gut. When you approach things, situations and people with an alert mindset, you will notice 'cues' you would never have noticed before. It will help you differentiate between honest people and dishonest people as well as innocent situations and not-so-innocent situations. It will be like your own 'mind reading' device that is built-in all of us.

Scientists refer to this internal 'mind reader' that we call our gut feeling as the subconscious mind. They also refer to our innate ability to quickly identify a dangerous situation that results in a fight or flight reaction as 'rapid cognition' or quick thinking. Scientists say that approximately 93% of our thought processes involves our subconscious mind versus only 7% of our conscious mind. This means that our subconscious is far more perceptive than most of us have ever imagined. At the least, we should all, undoubtedly, trust it. Our subconscious is able to see things, or hear, feel, smell and taste (the five senses) things that may cause an uneasy or gut feeling that we cannot consciously put our finger on. This can happen rapidly and, again, is called Rapid Cognition.

Rapid Cognition is, essentially, quick thought. Rapid cognition is the ability of all human beings to rapidly identify something that is important or unimportant to us and even rapidly identify something that is potentially dangerous to us. Rapid cognition, however, is difficult to use when you are surfing on the Internet or have let your guard down seeking romance online. To be better at using your rapid cognition ability, we recommend you use available information and 'red flags' commonly seen in dubious online dating, illegal Phishing emails and scam websites.

To name a few red flags that are good indicators of an online scam, whether it is dating or financial, we have listed them here by category for easy reference:

Red Flags in Online Dating

Online dating red flags are difficult, but not impossible to identify. As mentioned in more detail in a forthcoming chapter, one of the first red flags to be aware of is the 'rush to meet' note. This hasty or pushy attitude comes from someone who doesn't really care to get to know someone or someone who has limited time, such as a married person. In his early instant messaging or emails, the other person tries to rush you into meeting or 'getting together' way before the relationship has bloomed.

A bigger red flag is when that person becomes even more pushy and starts using sexual language. While it seems harmless because it is only online and the person doesn't really know who you are, it shows what type of person you are dealing with. Does he really want to get to know you or is he merely looking for an Internet thrill, fling or dirty talk? At this point, you should trust your gut feeling and end any conversation or contact with the 'perve'.

Phishing Scams

Phishing emails are extremely varied but usually carry one or more red flags of which you should be aware. The most common Phishing emails are the Account Alert emails. While some are generic in nature, others are specific and attempt to mirror popular Internet Service Providers (ISP), such as America Online, Gmail, Hotmail, or others. The red flags common among these phishing emails are misspelled words, immediate action requests, a click on their link leads to a website other than the name of the ISP, a request for your password or a request for your mother's maiden name and a request for your account number.

Phishing emails are sent out to the tune of several million per day and all across the world. Most likely, one of us is receiving one right now. Any email that 'wants' something from you should be carefully scanned for red flags. More red flags to look for are immediate action links (*Click here now*) like those explained in the Scam Websites paragraph coming up next and the use of poor grammar, foreign senders and multiple recipients. Phishing emails are usually sent out to hundreds, if not thousands of people at a time in the hope that a few victims are duped by the scam.

Scam Websites

Scam websites are usually full of red flags like "***click here***" buttons that don't work, or links you to other pages far different from the website you had originally intended to visit. And, with that said, NEVER immediately click on any link to a website or email because it could be linked to a site that could steal valuable identity data or passwords from your computer. Scam websites are usually created in the (mirror) image, or by using bits and pieces of, websites that are well-known.

Scammers also commonly use a technique called typo-squatting to direct unsuspecting victims to their websites. Typo-squatting is when a scam website is created by using common misspellings of popular websites, especially financial websites like PayPal and eBay. An example of typo-squatting of the popular website, PayPal is the intentional use of frequent typing errors made by Internet users, such as PayPak, PayPao, PatPal, PauPal, etc.... Another example is the way someone may misspell eBay when typing quickly, such as ebat, enay, and ebau. Typo-squatting relies on people typing quickly and carelessly or typing the wrong domain, such as *.com* rather than *.org*.

When you seek, and you find, trust yourself, trust your gut and make the right choices. There are usually red flags and they are commonly used by liars, scammers, other criminals and perverts. They do this to attempt to get unsuspecting people to do what they want. Their quest to obtain their dishonest benefit is usually evident in their words, actions and request for your actions. Heed it! Don't be fooled by it! In the forthcoming chapters, we will continue to provide information about online liars, dating scammers and other deceptions as well as how to conduct your own investigations to uncover and unmask deceivers.

Chapter 8

He's Persistent but is he Consistent?

Remember when the Internet first came into our lives, and brought so many wonderful things, such as music, relationships and new friends?

Think about the information we share on the Internet. Is it updated whenever there are changes in our lives? The short answer is NO. How many of you had a MySpace or Friendster account when they were the most popular social networking sites out there? You know, when everybody was doing it. Now, how many of you migrated over to Facebook when it became the most popular social networking site on the web? Lastly, how many of you deleted, updated, or completely changed your MySpace or Friendster accounts to reflect the same information you now have on your Facebook? Is the information consistent? Did you even remember you had a page? Some of you did, but many of you did not. That is where we come in. We will show you how to find this information online, on yourself and on someone you need to further investigate.

If we were to write down the thousands of stories about people who have had old profiles come back to haunt them, we could probably write an entire series of books on them, and keep the series going for years to come. The point is, this information is still there and will likely always be there unless you take active steps to remove it. Sometimes, even after you have taken steps to remove this information, you may still have issues. The point is to be careful what you post because one day someone may find that information and use it against you. From an investigative standpoint, old profiles can be a treasure trove of information. It can be used to understand who your target is, what are his old habits, who was he with, and when was he with them. You will find that some people have several accounts out there, one for friends, and another for his the alter ego, "Cassanova." Again, not to sound repetitive, the point is that this information is out there and can be found with the right tools. This brings us to our next topic.

Sources of Information

Before you can search for information on the Internet, you probably should have an understanding of some of the types of information that is available. Remember from our previous acronym, C-A-T-C-H, (Capture Assess Test Critique Hold), you will be **capturing** information on the Internet that you will later **assess** and **test** against your target.

For now, you do not need to learn any new phraseologies or acronyms, but only the fact that information tends to fit into generally two categories. These two categories are 'formal' and 'informal' information. We use these categories because they are easier to remember and provide you with a broad frame of reference where you will place the information once you obtain it. By citing whether something is formal or informal, you will know right off whether to trust the credibility of the information you have received.

When we talk about formal sources of information, we are generally discussing 'official' databases or catalogs of information that are deemed reliable based on the sources of that information. For example, earlier we had mentioned the inmate database, VINElink, which is an informational database that provides notice to victims and witnesses of crime when an inmate is going to be released from prison. We presume this information is credible because the information stems from inmate records, which are managed and updated by the State. There are many sources of formal information that are free to the public and readily available online. We will discuss some of the formal sources of information below.

Formal Sources

As we mentioned above, formal sources are generally deemed reliable because they tend to come from government sources or 'official' records managed by a public or private agency. Public records would fall into this category, and are considered just that, 'For the public'. Many States have enacted 'Open Records' or 'Freedom of Information' laws, which are based on the belief that all government operations should be 'transparent' and the records should be available for public inspection. The beauty of this act is that most, if not all, government records can be requested and viewed by members of the general public. There are sometimes administrative fees associated with these requests, but many States have adopted online databases where the information can be viewed online without being printed. There are many different types of information available out there, but you have to know where to look.

Public Records

Public records come in many forms depending on what you are looking for, and how quickly you want that information. One of the best-known public records systems are criminal arrest records. Think about those high profile cases on the news. How exactly does CNN or Fox News obtain the criminal complaint in the OJ Simpson case, and read the affidavit on television? Typically, news reporters will show up at the court where the affidavit was filed and request a copy of the complaint. It becomes a public record after it is filed unless it is sealed. You, too, can request a copy of a criminal complaint through your State's 'Open Records' or 'Freedom of Information' laws by asking the court for a copy. Now you are probably saying to yourself, "*I am not going to a court asking for criminal complaints and stuff, I don't want people to think I am a stalker.*" Fear not, that is why we have the Internet.

Online Criminal Dockets

Since the enactment of many of the 'Open Records' laws, many government agencies have begun the process of placing their court records online. The records include criminal, civil, and family court records that can be accessed online and in most cases they can be printed out. For example, in Pennsylvania, the PA Unified Judicial System has an online Web portal where you can conduct a search for information on a case (See Figure 7.1). The site not only offers information on criminal cases, but also contains civil dockets as well. You can search the site simply by knowing the person's name, or last name only with a first initial, and by providing a date range of when you want to search. This powerful search feature is fantastic for those of us in private investigations and now YOU can see it for yourself. Yes, you are welcome! If you own a business for instance, this information would be great when you are hiring new employees or conducting a background investigation.

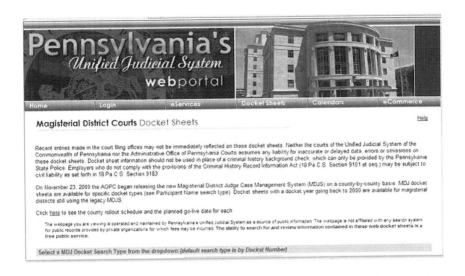

Figure 7.1 – PA Unified Judicial System Web portal

Online court dockets are not limited, only, to Pennsylvania. Many States have incorporated a similar database where you can search for information, for free online, with merely a name and date range. You will find that some states use different terminology to describe the participants in the case such as Defendant, Plaintiff, Participant, etc. These terms typically mean the same thing from State to State, but if you find a term you are not familiar with then we suggest looking it up in our glossary at the end of this book (See Appendix).

Professional Licensing

Another system that is considered a public record, and is available for public review is the State licensing records. Any professional licenses issued in your State such as medical licenses, nursing licenses, and others must be registered with the regulatory agency of that State. A simple search engine search and the state (Example: New York AND Medical Licensing = Results) will identify what that agency is in your home State. For Example, if we were searching in Texas, our results would suggest the Texas Medical Board where we can look up a physician (See Figure 7.2). Once you have identified that information, you can then search the database by name, address, or license number to determine whether that individual is indeed the professional he claims to be. You might be surprised to find out that your "Dr. Love" is not a doctor at all.

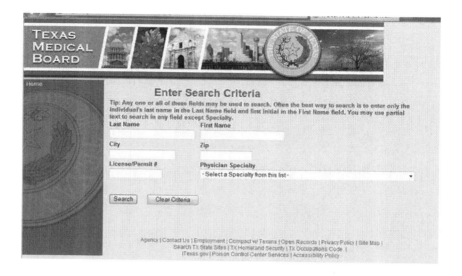

Figure 7.2 – Texas Medical Board Website

Another interesting fact regarding licensing records, which may not be related to dating, is whether this individual has had complaints or disciplinary action taken against him in the past. Most licensing boards will list any disciplinary action taken against a licensee (final adjudications only) and post it on their website under the license number. State Bar Associations also file information on attorney's, which includes complaints or other derogatory information, and can be easily found by the attorney's name. Again, you can fact check "Mr. Right", and make sure he is on the list. Additionally, if you are in search of a good attorney, the first place you should be looking is the state bar association.

Business Records

Remember our story about the woman who was conned into sending thousands of dollars in merchandise somewhere else using stolen credit cards? Well, part of what her online "Casanova" told her was that he was a business owner from of North Carolina and he needed her help sending out some merchandise while he was off to London with his ailing mother (who never existed). Unfortunately, our victim fell for the con. She shipped several thousand dollars worth of merchandise and almost ended up arrested because of it. Could she have prevented this from happening? Of course, by not doing it in the first place, and avoid all of the hassle. However, let's say this guy is "good," and still convinced her he is a business owner. How can we she check that?

It doesn't matter what type of business, if you want to operate anywhere in the United States, you have to register your business. Besides registering with the Federal government, all businesses are required to register in the State in which they are operating. Typically, this is done with the Department of State (not the Federal one) for each State under the Corporations Bureau or some other fancy name for it. For example, if you were in California you would search under the "business portal" for information on the suspect company you are looking for. Additionally, California gives you the option of searching by the "Director" or "Executive Officer" of the business, which is a nice feature especially if "Casanova" claims to be the sole owner (See Figure 7.3).

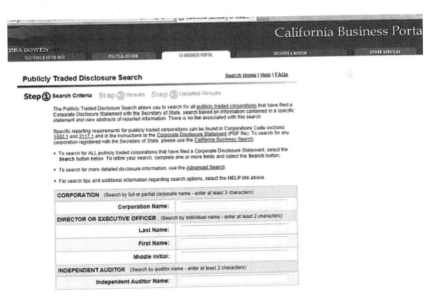

Figure 7.3 – California Business Portal

Many of these sites provide an abundance of information on the business owners themselves. We had once obtained the home address of a business owner, which he had registered with the State, and he did not realize this information was viewable by the public. Fortunately, for this business owner, we had revealed to him how easily we obtained his address, and he quickly resolved that issue by taking his personal information off the website.

Child Support Dockets

Everybody has heard of the phrase, "Baby Momma Drama!" This phrase highlights one of the most prevalent problems in relationships whether it is a serious relationship or simply a one-night fling. If there is a child involved (whether yours or his), you can probably guarantee there will be a significant other who may or may not want to let go (of him). Therefore, it will probably be a good thing to find out whether Mr. Right might have some little 'bambinos' running around. Moreover, if there are little 'bambinos' running around, what type of father is he? Does he take care of his kids? Better yet, are you concerned that the authorities will come bursting through your door to arrest him for lack of child support payments? Like the Apple iPhone there is an "App for that" too.

Online child support databases contain a wealth of information that can assist in your investigation. Think about it! What kind of guy doesn't take care of his kids, and will this guy do the same thing to you? These are questions you should be asking when you are delving deeper into someone's past. In Pennsylvania, the Department of Public Welfare manages the PA Child Support Program, which has dockets (court records) for child support, and domestic related issues. Our favourite, though, site is the Wisconsin Child Support Lien Docket (http://www.dwd.state.wi.us/liendocketweb). This site not only identifies individuals who are delinquent in their child support payments, but also gives the amount, and what agency is holding the lien (which gives you location). The records also include a date of birth, which can help you when you are searching for other information.

Tax Assessment Records – Real Estate

Real estate records are another excellent source of information when you are attempting to verify who owns what property. Within each municipality (county, city, township, borough, etc.), a tax assessment office or tax assessor analyzes all of the properties and valuates the property for tax purposes. As part of this process, the tax assessment office maintains records on all properties it assesses to include the dimensions, size of land, property owner, sale information, sale prices, and more. Sometimes, the tax assessment officers will have photographs of the listed property in their office. Probably the nicest part of all is that this information can now be found online.

In many States, the tax assessment office now has a searchable database online where you can enter an address, and look up who owns the property. Again, think of this in the context of what you are trying to accomplish. You want the truth. If Mr. Right claims to live at "XYZ Melancholy Lane" then his records should reflect that information. If you find that he is listed on the deed, and so is Mrs. Right, then there is a good possibility that you have just discovered a married man or he lives with his mother, which may be worse. Figure 7.4 is an example of the State of Maryland's Department of Assessments and Taxation, which shows that you can search for properties online through their portal.

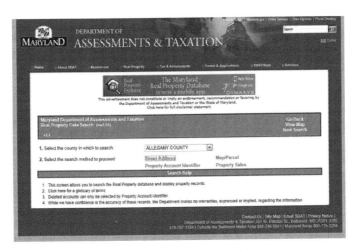

Figure 7.4 – Maryland Department of Assessment & Taxation

Commercial Databases

Much of what we have been discussing so far has entailed going out onto the Internet, and discovering information on your own. However, we would be remiss if we did not tell you that there are several companies out there like LexisNexis, Intelius.com, and others, who can do some of this work for you. The only catch is there is a fee associated with their informational products and depending on your budget, they can be very expensive. Our goal in writing this book is to help YOU become your own investigator, and seek out this information on your own. There are companies who claim they can do a background check on whoever it is you are looking at, but realize they are obtaining this information from the same sources that you can search for free.

Informal Sources

When we talk about informal sources of information, we are discussing those sources that may or may not necessarily come from a reliable source, but may be useful when combined with other information or when further evidence presents itself that corroborates this information. This information can come in the form of a blog, website, personal site, social networking, newsgroup, etc. Informal sources of information are one of the biggest concerns when it comes down to reputation defense, and 'old skeletons' appearing out of the closet (See Chapter 18 for more on reputations). However, informal information is where most of your investigative leads will take place. Do you suspect Mr. Right may be in a relationship? Is your spouse cheating on you? How many girls does this guy know? These questions can be typically answered through informal sources, which is why we are mentioning them.

Social Networks

Facebook, Twitter, MySpace, Xanga, LinkedIn, and similar sites are part of a category of websites called "social networking" sites. The value of social networking websites, as a source of information, can be the topic of an entire library of books. However, for the purpose of this book, we will cover the basic use of social networking sites as a source of information, and using that information in an investigative context.

The most popular social networking site out there is Facebook. OK, right now, as of this writing, it is the most popular social networking site in existence. The site touts a membership of over 400 million members throughout the world, and has become an online powerhouse. Think about it. How many people do you know have a Facebook account? Almost everyone nowadays is on Facebook, and businesses have recognized the potential of this exciting new medium. In fact, most businesses have a Facebook page where they advertise their wares, and ask YOU the consumer to 'Like' them online. This popular medium has resulted in a multi-billion dollar marketing industry that relies on the amount of information you post online, which is analyzed to target specific advertisements that you may be interested in. How do they come up with this information? They do so by what you post online, of course.

If you have a Facebook account, I want you to sign in, and look to the right of your 'Home' page. You will notice advertisements to the right of your home page that are consistent with the types of things you may have 'Liked' in the past, your friends may have 'Liked', or there are suggestions of ads you may be interested in based on your occupation, hobbies, etc. Facebook reviews your profile and determines the types of ads you may be interested in by using your personal information. It is no different from filling out a paper questionnaire and suddenly receiving junk mail in the mailbox from various companies based on your responses. The interesting part is many people do not realize how much information is too much.

As one of the largest social networking sites around, you can understand why it would also be a valuable source of informal information, and why we would talk about it in the first place. However, almost all of the social networks available operate in a similar manner. If someone sends you a 'Friend Request' you can review their page, and determine whether they are someone you know or just someone who may be interested in you. Before you accept that friend request, you better make sure you understand the ramifications of such a request. By accepting this person, you are not only giving him access to you, but many times you are giving him access to your friends, and your friend's friends. This is where we come in as investigators in search of the truth.

Browsing

Like most social networking sites, there is a search feature that allows you to 'browse' for friends that may have an account. Don't worry, if the people you know are not online yet, the websites normally allow you the ability to upload your contact list to see who may already be online or send them an e-mail suggesting they join. Even without an account, you can search for people and see if they have a page. This problem is one of our favorite features because it allows you to see their profile photo and sift through the various individuals who share the same name. Once you locate your target individual, you can open up his page, and review the information he has 'publicly' posted. However, if he is somewhat savvy about the Internet and privacy, you will find that he has limited some of his information to 'friends' only.

Browsing profiles is only one aspect of a social networking search. You can also search his friends or at least see who they are. This information is beneficial for many reasons because it allows you to see the type of people your 'Casanova' may associate with, or know. For example, does he have a lot of women as friends? What can you infer from someone who has over 400 friends, and most of them are women? I am sure you can make some assumptions about this individual based on this information alone. This is something we touched on in Chapter 4. The key here is that this information will help you build a profile of who this guy is, and why he is attempting to woo you in the first place.

Tagging, Time, and Location

Another valuable feature of social networking sites is the ability to 'Tag' a photo or location. Once an individual tags another individual on a social network he is indicating to the rest of the world two things, which are *"I know this person"* and *"here is a picture of him."* Although there is an ability to limit who can tag you in a photo, many people do not use this feature, and therefore are tagged by other individuals. This is beneficial to you as an Internet sleuth because you will be able to see the photo even if the person tagged has a private account, but the person posting the photo has a public profile. You will now be able to see a photo of your target and possibly any other acquaintances he may know (Male or Female).

Another aspect of tagging that many people are not familiar with is 'Geotagging'. Without going into too much detail, Geotagging' is when your location information is embedded into a photograph you take with a GPS enabled camera. When you take a photograph utilizing a smart phone or other GPS enabled device, the device captures location information, and inserts into the 'metadata' of the photo. We used this in our previously mentioned investigation in the beginning of the book. Using some free software, you can download this information, and learn where and when the photograph was taken. This information may be valuable if your 'Casanova' claims to be somewhere, but his photograph tells a different story. In fact, a website called "Icanstalku.com" attempted to educate the public about Geotagging by showing how this information can be exploited and why you should be aware this feature exists. An example of how this information can be exploited is clear in the story of the stalker who tracked his ex-wife to another state and showed up at her new, secret, home. She made the mistake of allowing her next door neighbor to post a photo of her and her children on the neighbor's social networking site. The husband found it by searching for her and the children and used the 'geotagging' information to find her. The rest is too horrible to recount.

When we talk about consistency, we generally are talking about information that may have been provided to you by the target and what his online persona may say. For example, whenever the authors are looking for social networking information about a target, we search all social networking sites to see if he has a profile on any or all of them. Oftentimes, people forget to update information or even delete an old account so that information is still available. It may provide some insight about whom we are dealing with. We have found an old MySpace profile on someone with various photos that may not be consistent with the Facebook profile he gladly volunteers to us.

Online Classifieds

Remember when classified ads were in the newspapers? The heading would read, "S/W/F looking for love", and there was a phone number where one could reach this "Single/White/Female" for a date. The phone number was also used many times as the number for a hoax, which would lead to a dating line. The Internet has changed the way we do classified ads by allowing someone to post a photo, add links, or even a personal website. Many of the dating sites you see online are nothing more than beefed up classified ads, but now there is a fee to watch (No pun intended). Craigslist is an example of an online classified site where you can buy and sell just about anything. And we mean ANYTHING! If you read various press releases around the country, you will see that sites, such as Craigslist, are often used for criminal activities such as prostitution, robberies, and the selling of stolen items.

Unfortunately, we have consulted on numerous cases where a victim's personal information was posted on one of these sites by a scorned ex-boyfriend who wanted revenge for a failed relationship. In fact, one victim, a High School teacher, had her information posted in the "Women Seeking Men" section of the local Craigslist personal ads. The advertisement invited men in our area to call our victim at her personal cell phone number "for a good time" and for "NSA" (No Strings Attached) sex. The victim received over 100 calls from a variety of men asking about the ad, and who now had the victim's private cell phone number. She was rightfully concerned for her safety and asked for our help. Fortunately, for the victim, we were able to track who posted the advertisement (which ironically turned out to be the ex-boyfriend), and arrested him for harassment and various computer related offenses. We also were also able to get the ad removed. This is only one of many stories involving the use of classified ads.

In the same manner that your information can be posted online, your target's information may also be online and ready for your discovery. If you suspect your "Casanova" may have an ad on Craigslist, we suggest running a search for his phone number or name. You can do this by using the almighty Google search, and the "Boolean" search techniques. Alternatively, Craigslist does have a search box where you can search specific ads for specific information. Some things to keep in mind, especially if your "Casanova" is Internet savvy, is he may post the phone number alphanumerically (both numbers and letters). For example, his number is 212-6667, but he spells it out as "Two-One-Two-Six-Six-Six-Seven." We have found that prostitutes also use this alphanumeric system to make it more difficult to search for specific numbers. Hey, we are not saying that the guy is a prostitute, but would you have known to do that?

Blog Postings

The Internet has opened up new ways of expressing oneself, and blogs have become a way that individuals can write out their ideas, which can be read by others in cyberspace. People share their thoughts on life, work, and sometimes anything that comes to mind. There are formal blog websites such as Wordpress, blog.com, and others. Some have even been integrated into news or other topical websites as added features. There are people who, now, are paid for blogging online and make a living off writing their thoughts. The use of blogs in any type of investigation cannot be overstated and there has been many instances where someone was caught because of an inappropriate blog or a comment from someone else on a blog. When searching for information on a blog, you want to pay attention to the followers, their usernames, and other identifying information. You will be surprised how this information can often corroborate other investigative findings.

School Alumni Sites

Part of the fascination of social networking sites was the ability to reconnect with people you have not seen in a long time. Think about it, Facebook started as a way for college students to connect online with each other and check their relationship status. Yearbooks were designed to memorialize our time in school and provide us with a 'photo lineup' of our former classmates so we can remember our friends, classmates, and other folks from our graduating class. We use the term "photo lineup" because we cannot count the amount of times we have used yearbooks to identify a juvenile offender who may not have a photo on file with the police. Now, you can conduct a search online, and look up someone from your graduating class through an alumni association website (See Figure 7.5). There are entire sites dedicated to this, such as Classmates.com and Mylife.com, providing the user with a quick and easy way to look up anyone online.

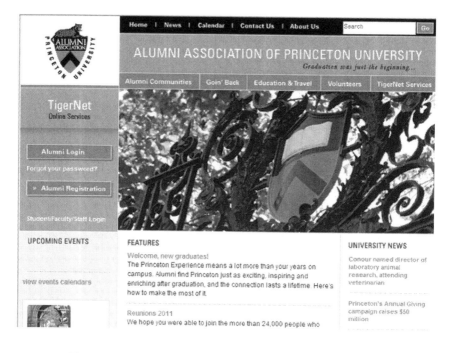

Figure 7.5 – Princeton University Alumni Association

In addition to finding this information, you will find that many people update their information on these sites and provide additional contact information that can be viewed online. We have found social networking information (profile info), e-mails, and even telephone numbers of individuals by simply searching for them on one of these school sites. The point here is that you are checking information that was initially provided to you during your initial 'Capture' phase. If he told you he went to a certain school, you should look it up. Additionally, you will find friends or former classmates who may be friends on his social networking site, which can give you access to his 'Tagged' photos. Do you see how it all goes together? School records are just one way to verify information and they can be used in conjunction with other information and to compile additional information.

Bad News, Good News, and No News

Another valuable source of information is local newspaper articles or stories about your target that may have been published somewhere online. Nowadays, whenever an article is posted from a major news source that same article is reposted on the Internet on various other news sites or mini-blogs that are published by various individuals for whatever subject they are writing about. For example, there are websites dedicated to the deaf and hard of hearing, which publish news articles about any issues affecting these disabled individuals. This typically includes articles about individuals who have abused a service that is normally dedicated for the deaf and hard of hearing such as 'Text-to-type services' and other forms of Internet services.

A simple Google search using the Boolean criteria we had discussed earlier should reveal associations and articles of interest. Once you have identified a potential article, you probably should verify the true source of it to verify its credibility. However, sometimes all you will have to go by will be the duplicated site because the source has either archived the article or is now requesting a subscription fee to access archived news articles. Remember that this information will be used to support your overall investigation and it is not necessarily critical if you cannot access the source article.

Who's watching who?

We would be remiss if we did not talk about whether someone can find out if you are searching for them online or gathering intelligence. Although the average user may not be savvy enough to realize that some things are traceable, a more computer literate person may be able to discern who has been perusing his or her profile. For example, if you are a LinkedIn.com user, you have probably seen the title "Who has viewed your profile" on the right hand side of the homepage. If you were to click on this header it will take you to another page, which shows you the individuals who have recently viewed your profile. You can see the name, photograph, when available, and industry that the person works in. From a networking perspective, this is great because you can connect with other like-minded professionals and share thoughts or ideas. For other people, it is a way of seeing whether you are being stalked online.

Unfortunately (or fortunately depending on who is looking), LinkedIn has also provided users with an option to browse profiles anonymously, which shows up as an 'anonymous' LinkedIn user on your 'Who has viewed my profile' page. If you are using LinkedIn to find information about someone, make sure you have selected the "Browse anonymously" option in your privacy settings. Another website, which also claims to help you find "Who has been looking for you?" is Mylife.com. Mylife claims if you become a member they will reveal who has been looking for you (provided they are also members of Mylife.com). Once you are logged in, you are given an option to connect with these members or invite them to Mylife.com.

In addition to the above sites, you must also keep in mind that many websites track who visits their sites either through capturing your IP address or by requiring you to identify yourself prior to using it. If your target is someone who is computer savvy and owns their own website, it is quite possible that they will know if you visit their website. So, tread lightly! When searching for information online you must ensure that you are doing it at a secure location and do not reveal any information about yourself. We suggest conducting most of your searches from an open internet connection like a coffee shop or other public internet access point. This gives you the anonymity of another IP address and makes it more difficult to track what you have done. However, if you are attempting to commit a criminal act, law enforcement will surely track you down regardless of your location. Other factors involved will signal to the authorities your identity, and you will be up that creek without a paddle. So don't do it! Don't do the crime!

There is a tremendous amount of information on the Internet, and too many resources to list in one place. The whole point of searching for both formal and informal types of information is to verify whether the information you have received is consistent with what you have found. The information we have provided you is only part of the equation. You have to decide what to do with this information and whether you can work with what you have found. Nothing we have talked about is secret. In fact, this is all public information and sometimes this information is better than a formal criminal history. What you do online can come back to haunt you. Beware! Actually, what you do online stays online forever, which we will discuss in the next chapter.

Chapter 9

What happens on the 'Net stays on the 'Net, FOREVER!

Whenever a discussion of the Internet occurs, several questions are always at the forefront of the conversation such as "Where does my information go once it is posted?" and "Is it secure?" The answers to these two questions are not a simple "Yes" or "No" because it will depend on various factors, most of which do not necessarily answer the question anyway. In a television series aired in May 2011, by the network CNBC titled, "Inside Google: The most powerful and successful technology company in the world", the host asks the CEO of Google, Eric Schmidt, about privacy concerns that some users have regarding the collection of the search information from its users. He confirmed that Google **does** store searches from individual users and the information is retained indefinitely.

After a certain period, Google anonymizes the information, which is supposed to shield the data that identifies a user. Of course, within the same episode, they expose a situation where anonymized results did, in fact, identify someone. Although to their credit, it was America Online (AOL) and not Google that was involved in that mishap. However, a good point is made in that interview. At the end of the day, it is personal 'judgment' that will ultimately decide whether your information is exposed, or not. That is, you will determine what type of information is out there based on what YOU post online.

Sometimes something as harmless as a family photo can become fodder for someone else or even serve as a marketing photo in a foreign advertisement campaign. In fact, that is exactly what happened to a Missouri family when they had posted a Christmas photo of their family on their website. A family friend had been traveling to Eastern Europe when he sees a billboard that was surprisingly familiar. The Czechoslovakian billboard, as it turns out, contained the family photo of his friends back in Missouri, which advertised an 800 number for some local service. In this circumstance, the use of this photo may seem harmless, but imagine how many other photos are out there that are being exploited. Like in the case of the woman who was searching adoption services when she saw her own seven year old son's photo listed on one of the adoption companies, purporting (at least through his photo) that this boy was eligible for adoption.

Can you imagine how outraged she was? And what kind of adoption agency steals photos of someone's child.

We have talked previously about the use of search engines in our investigations. Now let's talk about the available types of information on the Internet that you can search for, and for what purpose.

What's the 411?

Do you remember how you would look up a person's telephone number or address before the Internet? How about the phone number of a favorite restaurant or other business? There was a time when people would have to open a book (*I know, how ridiculous*!), about three inches thick, and sift through the pages to find the information they were looking for. Whether it was the "Yellow Pages", "NYNEX", or any other phonebook, you had to look through the various pages and find the information. Many times the information was alphabetized by last name or by category of business, but it was not an easy task. There also was a problem with the publication date of the document because of a change of number, private numbers, and businesses closing down. Finding the right phonebook that was up to date was always a problem

Today, we are fortunate that most of this information is now on the web and is easily retrievable by the click of a mouse. There are many sites out there that provide address and phone number information, and can be very helpful in your search for the truth. There are a couple of cautions that we must discuss right away so you are not misled by the information you are going to receive from these sites. First, sometimes this information is outdated or infrequently updated for many reasons. These reasons can range from the web sites administration to the owner of the information requesting they take down or remove this information from their site. Fear not! Outdated information may still be good information especially if you are doing a background check on somebody. For example, your target tells you he lived at "such and such" address, which was several years ago and you are able to corroborate this information by a simple search online.

Second, the information may not be there, which we alluded to earlier. In law enforcement, we are very concerned with officer's information being posted on the Internet for many reasons. There are several information sites out there that publicly post information on people without permission, and sometimes, as you will see, this information can be harmful. Many sites have a feature where you can request that your information be taken down for privacy reasons, depending on the type of job you hold (government service, etc). So, do not be discouraged if you don't find anything on these sites because chances are this information will be posted somewhere else.

As we mentioned earlier, in the 'old days' we would have to look up information in a book, but now we have the Internet. There are numerous directories online that have information regarding names, addresses, and sometimes, family members. These sites are known as 'People Locator' sites, White pages, Yellow pages (which is copyrighted), and 411 pages (from the old 411 information telephone service). There are international sites that provide telephone directories such as Infobel.com, and Wayp.com that provide information on almost 200 countries throughout the world. The usefulness of this information will depend on the accuracy of the website, and the amount of information the country in question allows the web site to collect on individuals. Europe, for example, has more stringent privacy laws than the US.

People locator sites can provide a significant amount of information on individuals, which include names, addresses, and sometimes phone numbers. One such site, Zabasearch.com, is a favorite tool for law enforcement, and is absolutely free (See Figure 7.1). In fact, according to the website the term "ZABA" is a termed derived from the Greek word "Tzaba," which means "Free" or "at no cost." The website provides you with several search options such as name or phone number, which can be broken down further by State. There are several free services available on the website, which includes people search, telephone search, IP address search, Zip code search, and even a FedEx tracking number (no clue why you would need this). Additionally, ZabaSearch offers some 'premium' services for a fee. However, as with everything else in this book, if you take the time you will likely find information you are looking for without paying for it.

Figure 8.1 – Zabasearch.com

When performing a search on ZabaSearch, pay close attention, not only to the address you are looking for, but also the associated addresses listed. There are many times when the associated information will prove to be more important than what you are looking for. One of our favorite discoveries is the names listed in the associated address fields. Look at the name. Is the name a female name? Is it a sister or girlfriend? Once you identify a name you will be able to look into that person and who knows what you will find. We will cover more of this in Chapter 21.

Another great site with many applications is Spokeo.com (See Figure 8.2). This site is classified as a People Locator that has many other benefits such as phone lookups, e-mail lookups, username lookups, and searches social networking sites for this information. The power of this little database is amazing, and it should be one of the first sites you look at when you are conducting an investigation. Spokeo is considered a 'Deep Web' search engine that can uncover obscure pieces of information not uncovered by other, non-deep web, search engines. Spokeo provides you with an easy graphical user interface where you can search by State, and then by locality on an easy to use map. Once you find this information, you receive some basic information and even a street level photo of the house (I know… scary! Thanks Google!). The premium services for Spokeo, which hover around $20 a year, can provide email addresses, phone numbers and additional family members living in the home (again looking for links). This is a great resource when you are looking for additional information.

Figure 8.2 – Spokeo.com Logo

There are several other sites dedicated towards 'People Locator' services such as Anywho.com, 411.com, and other sites. We suggest you use a well known search engine, and decide for yourself which one works best for you.

Photo and Video Sites

In addition to social networking sites, there are numerous photo and video sites out there that have a 'social networking' feel to them and can be used in a similar way. Flickr.com, Photobucket.com, Youtube.com and other sites have numerous photographs that can be searched online, and downloaded. You can search through these sites via a search engine or on the specific site themselves. Most photo and video sharing sites have a search field, which allows you to sift through photos and videos by topic, album, and the person posting.

The advantages of searching a 'photo only' site, depends on whether the site is associated with a social network. For example, Flickr.com is a product of Yahoo!, and you will find profile pictures on Flickr that are also posted in their social networking account. The advantage is sometimes even if the person's social networking profile is private, their Flickr account, which is automatically created when they start a Yahoo! account, may not be protected. Therefore, you are getting access to their photos and are able to review who is in them. Many sites offer similar services, so do not be discouraged if you find a social network that is private. Chances are you will be able to find something that they posted or linked to another account.

Criminal Records

In the previous chapters, we talked about the various sources of information available to you online. One of the formal sources of information we had discussed is criminal dockets or public court records. What you do, nowadays, stays online forever and can be searched by anyone at anytime. When researching criminal histories, you are not necessarily looking up whether somebody was convicted or not, you are attempting to develop a profile of the type of individual that you are dealing with. For example, if you searched your "Mr. Right" and noted in his history that he had a significant amount of Harassment, Simple Assault, or other assault charges, but none of them are "Guilty" convictions, what can you infer from this information? If you have a firm understanding of our criminal justice system then you know that most cases often result in plea deals for a lesser-included offense or the victim refused to cooperate. Now, we can understand someone being caught up in the moment maybe once, twice, but three times? You might have an issue that will rear its ugly head in the future. Remember that past behavior is often a good predictor of future behavior.

For more sites, and interesting search engines see the appendix.

Chapter 10

But his profile makes him sound dreamy: *I would love to know if it is true!*

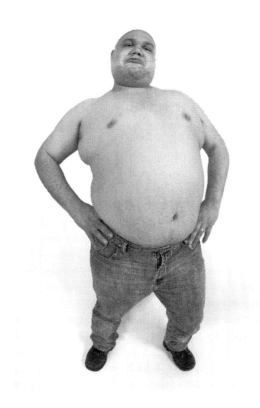

Identifying deception in electronic communications

Today's Internet is yesterday's street corner, nightclub and social meeting halls. We have said it so many times. What were once face-to-face meetings, or social gatherings, is increasingly being replaced with Facebook contacts, emails, chats, and text messages. What is so scary is how people can even fall in love with someone they have never met face to face. OMG, LOL, BRB...! WTF?

Even though it is, undoubtedly, much tougher to identify deception in someone's emails, it is quite possible to do so with a little 'detecting deception' know-how. **Now do we have your attention?** Deception and lying through the use of electronic communication, such as emails, has led to the biggest crime epidemic of all time, that is, of course, Identity Theft. If you have ever been online surfing the web or opened your email inbox you have a 99.9% chance of becoming, at the least, an 'attempt' victim of some form of Identity Theft. Words that were foreign to many of us a few years ago have become way too familiar. Words like phishing, pharming, denial of service (DOS) and urban legends have become part of our language and an everyday concern for Internet users, especially frequent Internet users.

Let's examine typical deceptions in emails, beyond the normal embellishment and bragging, and then get into what all you online daters are thinking about, *"Is he really for real?"*

Lying Online – The Use of Qualifiers

Typical deceptive language in emails is similar to deceptive language in face to face conversations. The use of qualifiers, such as *"This is so true, it really happened to me!"* is a common technique. The writer is trying to qualify what he is about to say and get the reader in a position to believe, or want to believe, what he is about to say or do. Just like when a liar says to your face, *"To tell you the truth..."* or *"To be totally honest..."* he is trying to get you to believe what he is going to say before he says it. There are many variations to this technique. Anytime you hear something like this, make sure you pay careful attention to the rest of the sentence and the person's story. Be very, very, suspicious of what comes out of his, or her, mouth, or keyboard next!

Fontacizing – Using Bold or Varied fonts and *Italics*

Another example of potentially deceptive language is the use, especially overuse, of emphasis for specific words or messages. These words will be *italicized* or written in **bold** or varied fonts. They are often surrounded by "quotes", or ending in exclamation points! Or even many exclamation points!!!!!!! The purpose is to get your attention and emphasize the message. It's a way of exclaiming when the speaker can't raise his voice or shout in your presence. Of course, being emphatic in written words, such as texts or emails, is not always a surefire way to identify a liar since many of us use it quite regularly when being truthful. However, when someone is trying to sell you something, online or in an email, pay close attention. Carefully scrutinize the entire message, especially when someone is trying to sell you HIMSELF!

In the example below, an email sent to a colleague of ours almost caused him to click onto a (hyper)link which would have made him susceptible to an online thief capable of stealing his personal and financial information. In this case of phishing, our colleague did his banking at the same bank used in the email. Of course, we have changed the email to protect our colleague and the real bank.

> **From:** Bank Fraud Department
> **To:** Banking Customer
> **SUBJECT:** Fraud Alert!
> Dear Banking Customer,
> It is extremely important for you to contact us **IMMEDIATELY.** Your bank account has been *compromised by fraud* and you are in jeopardy of **losing** future access to your bank accounts or, quite possibly, **a loss of money!** To save time, you **must link** to your account through our convenient account access portal provided here: **www.Bank.com/32456-%$#*&** .
> We thank you for your prompt action and are happy to serve you, now and in the future.
> Sincerely,
> Daniel Smith
> Fraud Examiner

This phishing email used many common methods for manipulating the recipient to do what the scammer wants. The scammer used exclamation points, *italicized* words, **bold words**, and a quick convenient (must) link to their site. To add to the urgency of the situation, the use of the bolded word **IMMEDIATELY**, attempted to push the recipient to act quickly. To go further, the scammer used scare tactics like italicizing the phrase "*...compromised by fraud*" and bolding the words "**losing**" and "**a loss of money**". In attempt to further influence the recipient into quick action, the phisher provided, as he put it, "convenient access" and "...to save time you **must link...**" He listed his convenient hyperlink at the end of the sentence that almost forces the recipient to 'click on it' with no turning back. Of course, the hyperlink directs the victim to a fake look-a-like website with blank fill-in fields asking for an account number, PIN, password and, most likely, social security number, mother's maiden name, billing address and home telephone number. Information like that can keep a 'phisher' busy for quite some time (making money through the victim's identity).

Emails – Too Much Information

A **lengthy email** is an indication of someone who is trying to convince or over-convince. In the field of detecting deception or exposing lies we call that 'giving too much information' or 'over expounding'. It is commonly used by liars to try to make a lie sound believable, especially when they don't believe it themselves. We have encountered many, many criminals during interrogations who use this type of 'lying' to try to convince us of innocence but it doesn't work because we are aware of the tricks.

Talking in Circles

Another example of deception, in texts, emails, IMs, etc..., like over expounding, is '**talking in circles**'. Talking in circles involves disorganized thoughts being exposed in long-winded or verbose text that always seems to come back to same idea. The writer can't seem to get away from it. It is a way to convince the reader that he is telling the truth or a way of reinforcing a statement that the writer really doesn't believe himself. It is common, today, in online dating situations. Talking in circles, in online dating situations, usually involves the same subjects: Sex, Marital Status and Trust.

The writer of the electronic message, usually a male, writes a lengthy message, or series of messages, to the recipient, usually a female, that may have one topic or several topics discussed but seems to always revert back to one of the three topics. In the following examples, once you are aware of the tricks, you can easily identify what the person really wants.

Example 1: "So Jen, how was work today? You must have worked your ass off because you didn't answer any of my texts. Poor baby! If I was there, I would have worked your ass. I hope you are not too tired to talk to me tonight online. I really want to spend some time talking to you. I want to finish our conversation about you, me and sexy music! What time do you think we can chat? I am free all night. I can be yours all night along, if you want it! TT4N."

How many times in his short paragraph did you find a reference to SEX? **ANSWER: 4**

Example 2: "Jane! Are you online? I have a few minutes! Can we chat! My ex is dropping off the kids before she goes to her 'crabby' mother's house. I miss you babe but this going through a divorce shit is taking too long. How was your day? I can't pick up while the kids are here so I'll text you when my ex picks up the kids. TTUL8R, Alligator!"

How many times in this text did you find him attempting to reinforce his alleged 'going through a divorce' situation? **ANSWER: 3**

Example 3: "Hey Sexy! What's shaking? I know you been buggin lately but I want you to know that you can chill on all that worrying. You the only girl for me! I told that chick not to call me 'cause I am in a serious relationship! Believe that! I want to CUL8TR after I drop off my boys around 11 PM. I want to show you this honest face and look into your eyes when you see how I really feel. I ain't like those other playas out there. I'm for real! For real for you! Miss you, baby!"

How many times in this text did you find him trying to 'over-convince' her that he can be trusted? **ANSWER: 5, 6 or 7.** And why does he want to see her after 11 PM? Hmm...?

Chapter 11

How to find out if Mr. Right is Mr. Wrong

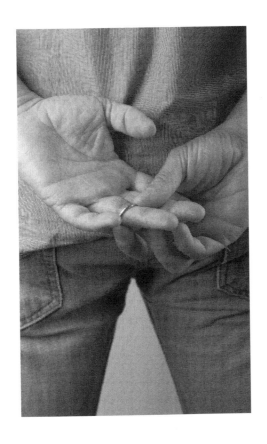

The anonymity of the Internet has made lying about one's 'status' very easy, and knowing whether someone is married or not is even more difficult since most profiles omit certain information. There are two ways to know if the person you are dealing with is married. First, ask him flat out and watch for signs of deception, like squirming, hesitation, throwing up, etc…, which will probably be the easiest method of discerning the truth unless he is a professional liar. (See Chapter 15 for more information on identifying lies and deception) Second, investigate him using your new investigative tools and see whether there is a leak online somewhere that can provide you with the truth. Obviously, we would want you to do the former first versus the latter, but we find the latter is more fun. It's always a good idea to be armed with information you uncovered online before you confront someone face to face or through some other direct approach.

Your first stop in any investigation into someone whom you suspect is married is official court records through your local Clerk of Courts or online court records. The act of marriage itself is a civil matter, which will be found in the civil division of most courthouses. Again, utilizing the techniques we have shown in the previous chapters, you can conduct a basic search of your target's name or the other person (woman) to see if their names appear on a docket. If you find a docket or license indicating the person is married, you can also check to see if the marriage dissolved in divorce, which, ironically, can be found online, too! For a fee, you can request copies of these records as they are considered public records and open to public scrutiny.

Another avenue, which is often overlooked, is your local newspaper marriage announcements. Open your local newspaper in the community pages and you will probably find marriage announcements of couples who have recently announced their engagement. The Internet has made announcements even easier within the online version of your local newspaper or separate community events page. A simple search engine query can reveal a past announcement with names of the individuals involved. Again, we are linking names, places, and dates, which will add to your investigation later.

Social networks are another way to identify a married person. We have found that married men and women often setup up two separate social networking accounts online, one with their family and friends, and one for fun. Typically, the main profile with the family and friends will have their formal name, John Smith, and the other site will have a past nickname or middle name as the main profile name. If you do not know this information then it is a good chance you will miss it. If you browse the social networking site for first names and middle names there is a good chance you will find the same pictures on both, minus the one with the wife, of course. Look for consistencies with the types of demographic information they post online, such as names, favorite activities, hobbies, etc.

An obvious area to check on a social networking website is the person's relationship status. A good indication that something is not right with a person's relationship status is when the person states, "It's complicated." We don't know about you, but we find some-one posting "It's complicated" as problematic. Either there is 'baby momma drama' or the person has some skeletons in the closet that he is subconsciously revealing. Remember Chapter 7 and the informa-tion about the subconscious mind. The answer to this question should be a straight forward, yes or no. In addition to indicating the person is in a relationship, you will find that they may also link the person they are in a relationship with in the same field. Therefore, you can click on the link, which takes you to the other person's webpage. How con-venient! Overall, social networks can provide you with a lot of good information. Look it over carefully and see what you get.

Most of the information from the previous chapters will assist you in identifying whether your potential date is married, or not. The key is to look for coincidences that appear to reflect a 'special someone' who happens to always appear in every search result. You might find that the person may be a former girlfriend or the baby momma. For obvious reasons, you may want to do some searching on this indi-vidual as well and see what you turn up. The goal is to rule out the possibility of a relationship by ensuring you know as much about this person as possible.

At the end of the day, if Casanova is good at the game then he will make sure that there is no trace of a current relationship either by outright lying or altering some aspect of the information he volunteers over the Internet. You must be able to sift through the nonsense and make sense of it. The broader picture of deception should be obvious and cause that gut reaction that something is not right. Trust your gut, and continue to process the information that you find. There is no doubt that he or she will slip up at some point, which will allow you to put the pieces together. When in doubt, check him out!

Chapter 12

Examples of Suspicious and Deceptive Language in Online Dating

> *"The problem with quotes on the Internet is that you don't know if they are genuine!"*
>
> ....George Washington

Many people are using online dating as a way to meet that special someone or someone to have fun with. Why not? Online dating has become extremely popular for singles with busy schedules, professionals, and single parents. It is extremely popular with people who don't like nightclubs, bars, or the traditional dating scene. Its convenience however, is equally exploited by cheaters, liars, and predators leaving some victims in the wake. Here, we'll expose one such person, as a way to make you realize, what type of person to be suspicious of while engaging in the online dating scene. Of course, not all online daters are cheaters, predators, druggies or outright assholes, but you need to be careful and aware. Now, take a look at this email that was generated to a friend from an online dating site:

> *From: SoulMateGuy420@_ _ _.com*
> *To: Jennie115@_ _ _.net*
> *Subject: The man of your dreams*
>
> *Hi Jennie! How have you been? I saw your profile on _ _ _ _
> _ _ _ _ and thought you are HOT! It took me quite awhile to get
> up the nerve to email you because I am really the shy, sensitive
> type but you are SOOOO gorgeous! Jennie, if it is OK with you,
> I'd like to tell you a little bit about myself. I am tall, athletic,
> and have dark hair. I have been told that I have rugged good
> looks. I am a corporate head of a Fortune 500 company and
> drive a sports car. I like long walks on the beach in the moon-
> light, with you, and believe in chivalry. I like, I am embarrassed
> to say 'romantic movies' and cry during the sad parts. I am
> looking for a friend and soul mate to share the good times, the
> bad times, and warm cuddling next to the fireplace. I am not
> into the dating scene or nightclubs but find myself seeking the
> companionship of someone to share life's special times with.*
>
> *So Jennie! Please WB and send me more pics of you. I have
> attached my photo in the sports car for your viewing pleasure.
> I AM SO LOOKING FORWARD TO HEARING FROM YOU, JENNIE!
> TTFN,
> Yours truly,
> SOUL MATE Guy (4:20)*

Now, let's analyze the email and expose the lies, misleading information, and deceptions:

Right off the bat, what kind of clown calls himself *SoulMateGuy*? Is
he really your soulmate? Was his screen name intended just for you?
Nobody else? Talk about someone trying to 'sell' himself. This guy is a
salesman! And *420*, is that his birthday? Is his real name, Adolf Hitler?
They have the same birthdate! Or is he so 'stoned' that he didn't think
you would realize that **420** is 'National Get High Day', commonly used
by stupid teenagers and 'weed heads'. We don't trust this guy already!

Subject: The man of your dreams

He is telling you, and probably every other girl he's emailed today that he is *'The man of your dreams'*. Talk about confidence and he thinks he knows your dreams. How self-absorbed is he? STRIKE TWO!

Hi Jennie! How have you been? I saw your profile on _ _ _ _ _ _ _ _ and thought you are HOT!

OMG, he thinks you're HOT! That may be true but he could have waited until the second sentence for the greatest compliment a girl wants to hear. Why didn't he think you are smart and nice and that you sound like fun? But he saw your profile with lots of words on it about who you really are but the most important thing (to him) was that you are HOT! STRIKE TWO!

It took me quite awhile to get up the nerve to email you because I am really the shy, sensitive type but you are SO gorgeous!

It took him quite awhile to get up the nerve to email you. Wow, your profile posted yesterday and he sent you a message within an hour. We would hate to see how long he takes when he is in a hurry. But then again, he is the shy sensitive type (that's what he said) but not too shy to say that you are HOT and GORGEOUS in the first 45 words of his first message to you. He's shy and sensitive but not shy and sensitive too much to refrain from being forward about telling you those magic words that every girl wants to hear...HOT...GORGEOUS. We don't trust him, but we'll hold off on STRIKE THREE just to be sure.

Jennie, if it is OK with you, I'd like to tell you a little bit about myself.

He wants to sell you, we mean tell you, about himself, if it's OK with you? Is it? Did you answer him or is he retarded? Let's find out about what he says about himself. We are sure it is the truth. Or is it?

I am tall, athletic, and have dark hair. I have been told that I have rugged good looks. I am a corporate head of a Fortune 500 company and drive a sports car.

Are you getting this? He's tall, athletic and he has dark hair! Nice!!! What does athletic mean? He looks like he works out? Like he runs a marathon? Sumo wrestlers are athletic, aren't they? I think we need more information. But he is a corporate head for a Fortune

500 company and he drives a sports car. How lucky are you? Call your mom! Tell her you met your soul mate and HE IS RICH!!!!!!! Hey, wait a minute! Don't call her yet! Is a Miata a sports car?

I like long walks on the beach in the moonlight, with you, and believe in chivalry.

OK, we just finished puking but is he kidding? Long walks on the beach have been used 45 trillion times by guys looking to get laid. Now, we think he is really full of shit! But he wants to lake long walks on the beach with YOU so he must be a good guy then. NOT! He believes in chivalry! What does that F&%$&#@ mean? Is he going to place his royal shawl across the surf during your long walks on the beach together? Or is he going to protect you from the evil men out there across the world (wide web) seeking to deceive you just to get in your pants? You're not falling for this crap are you?

I like, I am embarrassed to say "romantic movies" and cry during the sad parts.

Oh no he didn't! Yes he did! He said he likes "romantic movies ". If he likes them, why is he embarrassed to say it? Is he lying? Yet, he's not embarrassed to admit to crying during the sad parts. We're confused! No we're not, he's a scammer!

I am looking for a friend and soul mate to share the good times, the bad times, and warm cuddling next to the fireplace.

We think we can translate this one. HE WANTS TO GET INTO YOUR PANTS!

I am not into the dating scene or nightclubs but find myself seeking the companionship of someone to share life's special times with.

We think he should have deleted the entire message and only used this line. Even we would have been tempted to believe him and we don't believe anybody online until we meet them face to face!

So Jennie! Please WB and send me more pics of you. I have attached my photo in the sports car for your viewing pleasure. I AM SO LOOKING FORWARD TO HEARING FROM YOU, JENNIE!

Well, at least he attached a pic of him in his SPORTS CAR, for YOUR VIEWING PLEASURE. We thought he was shy and sensitive! He sounds overly confident you are going to like the picture he took out of a GQ Magazine to pass off as him.

TTFN,

Yours truly, SOUL MATE Guy (4:20)

OK! We've had it! STRIKE THREE! What kind of self-respecting male says Ta Ta For Now (TTFN)?

Everyone should be suspicious, and aware, of someone trying to sell themselves too much in their profiles and emails. Yes, it's a sales pitch like a used car salesman would use. But, be especially aware of hints into the person's habits or practices like the use of 420. 420 is commonly used, as we mentioned, by teenagers and people who smoke a lot of weed (marijuana). Using 420 in his screen name, unless he is a fan of the Columbine HS Massacre which occurred on 4/20/99 and a neo-Nazi fan of Adolf Hitler, is probably an indicator this guy is getting stoned all the time and could not be the corporate head of a Fortune 500 company. Maybe he is all three! Click DELETE!

Chapter 13

He dates online often. *How Many Girls? OMG!*

It seems that nowadays, the measure of a person's popularity is the amount of people following them or the amount of friends they are connected to. However, when does the amount of friends someone has become an indication that they may be a little too friendly with the opposite sex? The obvious answer may be when 300 of his 310 friends are all women who appear to be a little too casual with him. If only it would be that easy. Imagine if there was one location where hundreds of his prospective dates are seen in a single location. We highly doubt that these women would be too fond of a man who has this many female friends. What about the Internet dating game? Can you tell if your Mr. Right may, in fact, be Mr. Two Times or Three Times over? Probably. But you have to look around first.

There are many popular dating sites out there, which include everything from Christian dating sites to sadomasochistic dating sites where you can find a partner to spank you while you are wearing a pair of adult diapers. We are not kidding, it is out there, so we heard...wink. Most people either try several dating sites before they decide to quit the online scene altogether or find a particular site that is appealing to them and stick with it. It is possible that you will find your Casanova on several sites "looking for love" and that would be fine. However, if your Casanova has a profile on Christiansingles.com, and you also find a profile for him on Adultfriendfinder.com, needless to say, something is not right. One site seeks out companionship based on the principles of Christianity, and the other is for people who are looking for NSA sex. Your radar should be sounding the alarm at this point because your possible match may be a 'Player' or a 'Freak'.

Now, we are not saying that someone could not have converted to Christianity and forgot about their former profile on the other site. But this is not a good sign to start with and can be indication of trouble. Are you one of many conquests for this guy? How many websites is this guy on? Is he a professional online dating machine? There are several indicators you might want to look for in a profile, which may cause concern about his behavior, and re-evaluate whether this guy is truly in it to find true love or true love for only one night. The choice will depend on what YOU are looking for on these sites. You have to decide how much you are willing to take and how far you are willing to take it.

The Professional Profile

How do you know when someone is really good at this online dating thing? By looking at the profile information of course! How much information is this guy revealing in his profile? Is he using acronyms or Internet slang unique to online dating? For example, does his profile say: *"MSW seeking Sub to have NSA sex, and BDSM on the weekends. Send a BBM or MMS me. LNK."*

The preceding profile text means: *"Man seeking Woman who is seeking submissive to have no strings attached sex, and bondage, discipline, and sadomasochism on the weekend. Send me a Blackberry Message or Multimedia Message. Love and Kisses."*

We don't know about your online dating history, but we are sure that you did not know what all of these acronyms meant or at least you had to look a couple of them up before you started using them. The point we are making is that this guy is no stranger to the Internet, and even more so, to the online chat scene. This guy knows how to communicate on the Internet and knows what he is looking for. Would you respond to a profile with this kind of introduction? IDK... maybe, or hell no! It depends on what you are looking for, doesn't it?

The second item you should always evaluate is the profile photo. What does it show you? Is it different for each site? Does it show varying degrees of personality? Would you check out a guy if he was wearing a bondage mask in all of his profile photos? If you do, we won't judge you. Or does the guy pose in his Christian dating account with a bible in his hand, and on the other site he is shirtless with a bottle of Jack Daniels in his hand? Again, you should be looking for inconsistencies in the profile. It's an indication that this guy is cruising for some 'booty', so to speak. Look at the photos and analyze whether he is presenting the same image throughout or altering his appearance to fit the situation.

Another interesting aspect is the reviews people post about dates they have had online. One such site, www.abadcaseofthedates.com, is an interesting site where people post some of the bad dates they have had from online dating. We suggest you review these sites, and see if your Casanova is mentioned. You would be surprised on some of the similarities between the experiences other people have had and your own. A simple Google search with your prospective mate and the words "Bad Date" can turn up some interesting stuff. Overall, if you want to find out if Mr. Right is Mr. Popular then conduct your standard searches, and analyze what type of information he provides in his profile. Be careful with the professionals, as they know how to hide their information, and speak in code. It can turn out that you may not be ROFL (Go ahead, look it up in the glossary at the end of the book) about being one of many of his conquests.

Chapter 14

Online Dating Behavior that Tells You to "PROCEED WITH CAUTION!"

In the following examples, try to identify how many times you've encountered these 'lines' or 'behavior' from a potential date. Possible explanations of these behaviors, though speculative, are offered solely for your awareness and protection.

CHATS and EMAILS

Rushes to meet you in person. When the online relationship is in the very beginning stages, it is probably not a good idea, for a few reasons, to rush meeting someone in person. Getting to know that person better is probably the best reason. While someone rushing to meet you in person might merely be someone seeking to advance the relationship quickly or just someone who is anxious to meet you, it can also be an indicator of someone who wants to minimize his online time for fear of getting caught by a significant other. He might also be someone who has limited time to meet people in person, like a married man, work release inmate or a speed dater..

Pushy. Tries to push or influence you into something you are not ready for by making conversation that is right to the point, yet too soon. When someone makes attempts at sex talk in the beginning of an online relationship it shows that that person is pushy and it should make you concerned.

Beats Around the Bush. Instead of being specific or to the point about issues or his agenda, he is vague and non-specific. He may be trying to be too cautious or non-committal. Also he may want to get you to say something first or does not want to be offensive.

Edgy. He sounds like he is on edge or nervous. That person may be cautious because he is fearful someone else is watching (him online) or may see his writing. The person may just be having a bad day.

Impatient. The person steers the conversation to a quick fruition rather than taking his time. He may be in a hurry to get to the point because he is insincere or has limited time to have a conversation. Usually, that is an indicator of someone who does not truly care about what you have to say.

Sex Talk Online Immediately. Anyone who engages in sex talk in the beginning of an online meeting or relationship is clearly out for one thing!

Inappropriate language. Uses explicit language or sex talk when the relationship is new or 'not at that point', yet. Inappropriate language is often used by someone who surely does not respect the other person, or he only cares about having sex, online or in person.

Overly Romantic. When someone sounds too romantic for a new online relationship, especially when you have not met, it should be cause for concern. Why is this person doing that? Are they preying on you to get you to do something you am not ready for or something that may be improper or illegal. Online fraudsters use the 'overly romantic' tactic as a way to get innocent online daters to unwittingly take part in their schemes of identity theft, credit card fraud and nude photos or sexual videos or conversations to sell them to sex sites.

Asks for revealing photos. Revealing photos sent to someone online, especially someone you have never met or know intimately and thoroughly, is just plain NOT SMART. Never send anything to anyone online that you don't want the whole world to see FOREVER. Remember, in the previous bullet how photos and videos can be sold to sex sites. You may see yourself online someday, or worse, your parents may see you!

Brags about Sexual Prowess. Anyone who brags about his sexual prowess, without a doubt, is insecure, or, worse, a sexual predator. Anyone who is respectful of the other person is going to steer clear of such behavior.

Avoids Conversations About Current Relationship Status. When someone is trying to narrow the other person down about his current relationship status and that person attempts to avoid the conversation, there is reason to be concerned. There is an old online saying, that I just made up, that goes like this, *"Someone who can't commit about his commitments can't commit because he is probably already committed!"*

Inconsistent Statements. What a tangled web we weave when first we practice to deceive. People who weave tall yarns about themselves and their life, unless they have carefully planned an intricate cover story, often show inconsistencies in their statements to others. This is a clear indication of deception and a person not to trust.

PROFILE

Non-committal about Family Status. Profiles usually have two choices. Those choices are Married or Single. When an online dater uses Separated, Divorced, Not Living at Home or some other word, it should raise an eyebrow or two, unless you have a unibrow and then you will only raise one. Your only one!

Vague Self–description. When someone describes himself in a way that it is difficult or impossible to visualize, that person might be purposely providing a vague self-description. There could be a host of reasons for this, such as fear of being identified by the police or maybe the person is trying to sound appealing to a wide variety of the opposite sex, or same sex, but it is suspicious. A vague self-description is a good indicator of someone who does not want you to know what he really looks like. Ask for a recent picture of him, showing head to toe, holding today's NY Times (With the date visible).

Non-Descriptive Words. Use of words like athletic, well-proportioned and needs to lose a few pounds all sound like someone who is endowed (What are you thinking of?) with an attractive physique but it also may be hiding some important information. What does athletic mean? Is it good for a woman to be athletic or is it just for a man? And how many pounds does someone need to lose when he says "needs to lose a few pounds"?

Non-Specific Job. But what does he do for a living? Is he an Account Executive? What the F%$#$ does that mean? Is he a VP of Technical Services? More confused! And what the heck does self-employed really mean? Non-specific job descriptions can be a vague indicator that he is trying to hide his real job due to having a job that is not typically attractive or usually doesn't make that much money. We believe, wholeheartedly, especially in the dating world that honesty is the best policy.

Non-specific Place of Residence. Surely we can't expect someone to list his full address on his profile but when the relationship develops past the *"Hi, I'd like to get to know you!"* phase, it's time to be more specific. When someone lists 'Chicagoland area', it can mean anywhere in Chicago and the dozens of cities and counties surrounding it, even as far as the Wisconsin. The same thing goes for L.A. (Los Angeles). Los Angeles can mean Los Angeles city and even Los Angeles County which covers dozens and dozens of cities and towns or the areas close to LA County. Why would someone list a non-specific place of residence, you ask? We think most people feel safe in the anonymity of the Internet and the Online Dating scene but there could be a variety of reasons. One reason could be they don't want someone driving by their house after searching and locating their address online, even though, as you will learn later in this book, you can trace someone's IP Address through their emails and pinpoint them to the closest server near their home. (See Chapter 21 to learn how search someone's IP Address) Another reason can be to keep their true residence location a secret due to existing relationship(s), additional online dating endeavors, criminal intent or other nefarious reasons.

ONLINE ACTIONS

Abrupt or Frequent Shut Downs (Going Offline) During Online Conversations. When you are exchanging live emails or chatting online, even texting, and the other person goes offline or you are unable to reach him for quite awhile, it could be innocent. But when it happens abruptly and often, it may mean that person had to shut down because his wife, significant other or kids walked into the room or are snooping. Frequent shut downs, without reasonable explanations, should make you suspicious. Of course, he could be telling you, truthfully, how terrible his Internet and cell phone service is resulting in frequent shut downs but he could also be LYING!

Changes Screen Name. People don't usually change their screen name, although they may change their ISP for a better deal. Screen names become a person's identity. It's their online persona. Some people use their childhood nicknames while others use their screen names as a nickname. There was this guy who used the screen name '*BigGuy1010@_ _ _ .com*' who insisted he be called BigGuy all the time. He was 5'3" tall. AYLYAO? When someone changes his screen name, there is usually a good reason or there might be a suspicious one. A good explanation is because he changed ISPs and couldn't get the same screen name and a suspicious explanation is he was tired of the screen name and wanted to try something different. It could be legit but we doubt it!

Changes ISP Often. Online users may change their ISPs but changing it often causes loads of inconvenience. Loss of email history and contact lists is just two of the problems. So why would someone change his ISP often? One reason to change your ISP often is because he was thrown off of an ISP for 'bad behavior (explicit language, too many complaints against him, failure to pay ISP fees, etc...). Another reason to change an ISP can be related to the need to be anonymous, distance himself from previous contacts, or simply create a new online identity. Why would someone need to create a new online identity? We are sure you can think of several additional reasons by now!

MEETING IN PERSON

Asks You to Meet at His Hotel Room. Why would anyone meet someone for the first time in a hotel room? And what kind of person would ask someone he never met in person to meet him at a hotel? Someone who is aggressive or presumptive (looking to get some action) that's who! Oh, and serial killers, rapists, kidnappers and weirdos do that too!

Wants to Meet in Obscure, Undisclosed or Faraway Places. Convenience and safety for both parties is usually the location of choice for people who met online to meet in person. When the other person chooses an obscure or faraway location like a secluded National Park or someplace that takes a long time to get to, it's strange and should be unacceptable. And what about if he asks you to meet him in an area so you can travel to another undisclosed location? In that case, he is either cheating or he is going to make soup out of your bones! Does the name Jeffrey Dahmer come to mind?

Meets for a Quick Cup of Coffee or Brief Meeting in Bars, Parks or Playgrounds. Meeting for the first time for a quick cup of coffee is not uncommon today but when it happens more than once, it may be indicative of something else. Maybe he is juggling several dates or relationships or maybe his relationships are too costly and he is broke! Meeting at a bar is impersonal but it also affords him the opportunity to ditch you if he doesn't like what he sees or hears.

Meets You Near His Place of Employment, Not Near His Home. Of course, meeting near work can be convenient for both of you but it can also keep him from being seen by someone like his wife, in-laws, friends or others who may be appalled by his dirty little secrets. Many 'cheater' relationships start at work and many more are facilitated by hooking up near work. It affords cheaters ease of access, anonymity, knowledge of the area's obscure rendezvous spots and a good excuse like working late!

Avoids Meeting You in Person. Unless he clearly shows you he is exceedingly busy or out of the country, avoiding a face to face meeting is suspicious. While you may be at the point of meeting in person, he seems to be avoiding, or postponing, such a face to face meeting. This may be in an indicator of someone who is already in a relationship or does not want you to see what he really looks like.

Chapter 15

More Lie Detecting and other (online and offline) Deceptions

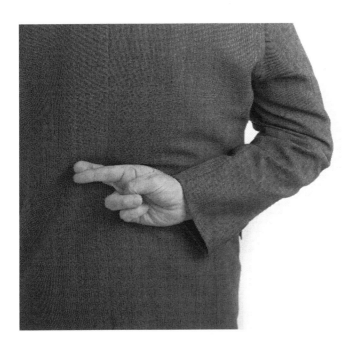

Liars lie, not all the time, but the more they lie the more they 'get over' on people. The more they get over on people, the easier they find it to lie and probably, the more they lie. Their lies, however, make them easy to identify when you know what you are looking for. Liars are mostly identified in face to face contacts and sometimes, even in the analysis of their handwriting, but what do you do when you have not gotten to the 'face to face' contact and you haven't hired a hand-writing analysis expert? And who writes letters anymore?

When you can't see someone's face to discern their facial expres-sions, decipher their body language or watch the physiological changes that occur in someone who lies, pay close attention to what is said, what is not said and how it is said. The following are good indicators of deception in written and verbal communication, whether online or offline!

Incongruence

Experts say incongruence is the most accurate way to identify deception and lies. Incongruence is the inconsistency in a person's statements, word choice, voice inflections and body language. In other words, when someone is making a statement, his/her statement should be consistent with the choice of words, voice inflections and related body language. In the world of online dating, when a potential suitor makes the following statement in his email, certain incongru-ence tells you he is not telling the truth or merely being deceptive. Either way, you shouldn't trust the statement as fact. Try to find the incongruence (inconsistencies) in the following message yourself!

> *"Hey Babe! What's new? I haven't had a chance to get online in the last few days due to a busy work schedule. But I wanted to see how you are doing. I've been under the weather lately but I have some time to spend with you now. Can we chat tonight? Hopefully between midnight and 1 AM????? I'd like to talk about us! CUL8R.....*

Did you see them? How can someone who has been under the weather, which usually means 'sick', have such a busy work schedule? That's inconsistent! And what about chatting between midnight and 1

AM? That's abundantly incongruent with someone who says *"...I have time to spend with you..."* No doubt, the use of the word *"Babe"* and the phrase *"I'd like to talk about us!"* is exceedingly incongruent with someone who has been out of touch for a few days and can only chat after midnight! LIAR!!!!!!

Lack of Emotion

A common indicator of lying is the lack of emotion in someone's story. People who lie tend to leave out emotions while truthful people normally refer to emotions in their stories. When someone lives through an incident or situation, that person will relive the emotional experiences consistent with the incident and refer to them in his explanation. Liars, because they are fabricating information, leave out emotions typically related to a truthful explanation.

Lack of Details

Liars also tend to leave out details because they are creating information that is not true. People who are telling the truth will refer to details that are consistent with their experiences. An example of this is a person's explanation of their last night's experience. A truthful person will mention specific details related to the circumstances that occurred during their last night experiences while a deceptive person, a liar, will be vague or fail to mention details.

Immediate Repetitive Words

Immediate Repetitive words can show careful thought or fabrication. Immediate repetitive words are often used in deceptive emails, instant messages, or other written statements. This is commonly seen in the use of words like "the the", "I I", "and and" or "that that". This is a good indicator the writer is taking careful thought in his/her written statement and the first word (the the) was already forgotten about resulting in a duplication of the word. This occurs because the person is moving from one thought or memory to creating, or fabricating, another thought (lie) that requires such careful contemplation that he forgot where he left off.

Soft Words

Soft words, also referred to as 'avoidance words', are frequently used by liars to minimize the severity of something that was done, for example the use of the word 'died' rather than 'killed'. Killers often use the word 'died' when they refer to the person they 'killed' in order to minimize the death of their victim and to minimize their own responsibility. In online dating, a potential romantic suitor may use the word 'separated' for their marital status when, in fact, he is still married. An appropriate, honest, marital status should be listed as 'single' or 'married'. Another example of a soft or avoidance word in the online dating world is when someone uses, "I'm tied up!" when asked the following question: "What are you doing now?" He is avoiding giving a truthful, straightforward answer. Why is he avoiding the answer? Is it because he can't tell you what he is doing right now? Is he doing something you would not approve of?

Changes the Subject/Avoids an Answer

Liars avoid being pinned down into providing information that can be detrimental or 'damaging' to their reputation or information that is not favorable. To avoid this, liars will segue into another topic or simply change the subject. Here is an example:

> **Instant Message from Darla to Johnny:**
> *"Hey Johnny, what time did you get home last night? I tried to reach you on your phone but I got your voicemail!"*
> **Johnny's Response:**
> *"Darla, yeah... I was working late but I got you something that I know you'll love!"*

As you can detect, Johnny avoids answering the question by changing the subject and segueing, or transitioning, into another, unrelated, topic. He even goes beyond that by telling Darla he got her something to further distract her and make her forget about the original question.

Avoidance of Guilt

Liars refuse to take responsibility for their actions and avoid making statements that may implicate themselves in wrongdoing. Truthful people make statements even when it shows guilt or responsibility for something unpopular or essentially wrong. The truth is the truth, even if it shows culpability.

Too Plausible

Truthful people provide information or tell a story whether it makes sense or not. The truth is the truth, whether it makes sense or if it doesn't make sense. You can't change the truth. Liars go to great lengths to make their lies to make sense or sound plausible. In an attempt to sound believable to the person they are speaking to, in this case online writing, liars can be very careful to try to make their explanations or stories make sense.

Dead Air/Stalling/Hesitation

During chats, texts and instant messaging and even emails, a prolonged stretch of 'dead air' may be an indication of stalling or hesitation. Stalling or hesitation is common when someone is attempting to create an answer that is plausible or one that sounds reasonable. The lengthy 'dead air', which may be more than slightly longer than usual, gives the person a chance to think of something to say. Liars frequently use 'dead air' as a way to stall their responses and fabricate a statement that can satisfy the question or minimize the damage.

Being able to tell the difference

Discerning between truth tellers and liars can be the difference between dating a married man and a sincere man of your dreams. It can also mean the difference between hooking up with a nice guy and the Craigslist killer. Pay attention!

Chapter 16

Text, Lies and Videotape:
Social Networking Lies

Tweet on Twitter, show your face on Facebook, get face time on Face-Time, have friends over to MySpace and see you on YouTube. What a great way to socialize! How much fun it is and how exciting to network, e-socialize and e-everything. Social networking is our new way of life.

In these modern times of social networking sites and social inter-action online, it is often overlooked that those we socialize with or the social network itself may be less than truthful in their representation of themselves, their experiences, and their business practices. Social networking has become the modern street corner and the modern coffee shop. Face to face, personal, interactions are increasingly being replaced by online electronic connections. People are linked-in, connected, and e-socializing but the fact remains there is no replace-ment for real-life face to face human interaction, especially when you want to know if that person is being sincere and honest. And when the person you are interacting with is a potential friend, a potential lover, or a potential business associate, it is exceedingly important.

So much business, dating and other daily interactions are done online that it is in everyone's best interest to better understand what they are really getting involved with when engaging in social network-ing. Let's try to examine the way, type and reason people and the social networks use lies in social networking.

Social Networking Lie Number 1: *Facebook Friends*

I have <u>85</u> friends. Obviously, that's a lie. While someone can have that many friends, can they really find so many friends that also have 'no life' that they can be on their Facebook page, too? Oh... sorry for offending you Facebookers. No, it's really cool to be on Facebook. I mean it! You DO have a life...on Facebook. Are they really friends like the ones you can count on or are they just acquaintances? If they are just acquaintances, then the amount of friends is a lie! Ok! That's not a big deal and we all get the Facebook friend's thing, we think!

Well, if someone has so many friends on Facebook, he must be a great person. All those people can't be wrong, especially that guy Tom, he's on everyone's Facebook page. If he is there, this guy must be grrrreaaat! That many friends, when they are not real friends who people know personally, lend itself to deceive people that the person they are e-socializing with is a good and trustworthy person. It may be quite the opposite. Anyone who allows that many people into their personal information, children's photos, conversations and other friend's lives is probably too naive to trust, anyway.

Social Networking lie Number 2: *Kids under 13 can't be on Facebook, MySpace or Twitter, or Xanga, Friendster, or some two hundred other social networking sites.*

We all know that's not true and if you have children like we do, you know that many of your kid's friends, even those as young as seven, have Facebook, MySpace and other social networking pages. Some have parents who have clear heads and other's (kids) just lied to set them up.

Social Networking lie Number 3: *"My social networking is safe!"*

Now that's a lie. While many people try to keep their social network pages private, they can't guarantee that everyone on their page is safe to them and everyone else. Social networks, with their facilitated anonymity and ease of posting someone else's pictures, someone else's pedigree and just plain posing as someone else, cannot guarantee safety. And then there are the criminals who use social networking to locate victims and find out when they are away from home.

In September of 2010, a burglary ring was busted by police in Nashua, N.H. Police said they terminated the crime spree of a burglary ring in which the three suspects targeted Facebook users who posted their locations. They committed more than 50 break-ins while homeowners were away, and police recovered more than $100,000 worth of property when the suspects were caught. What social network users need to remember is that geo-tagging provides their location in their postings and the text they provide gives criminals information they need to know when victims are away from home. And tweeting that you are away from home makes you a TWIT!

Social Networking Lie Number 4: *Online Flirting isn't Cheating*

So you flirt with this girl online that you have never met face to face. That's cool. But will your wife think it's cool? I doubt it! And have you told that online girl you have been flirting with on Facebook that you are married or merely that you are separated? No matter how you look at it, it's flirting. Online or not online. Most of us think its cheating!

Social Networking Lie Number 5: *What happens in Our Social Network, Stays in Our Social Network.*

Gossip, lies and videotape...and photos, too. We share it in our network only with those who are part of our social network. We hope! And the people we share it with will keep it, you know, just among us friends. It's confidential, it's our secrets. Or we hope so. Remember what we said in Chapter 9, *"What happens on the 'net, stays on the 'net, FOREVER!"* It's easy to post information on the Internet, even in a social network, and it's even easier, if you know what to do, to take that information out of the social network. The truth is, so much information passed on between fellow networkers is taken out of the network and passed on to others. And, don't forget, the social network itself has access to all your information, conversations, photos, videos, postings, and everything else. OH, that's right - they couldn't and wouldn't do that! YES THEY CAN AND WILL!

Social Networking Lie Number 6: *My Social Network Friends can be Trusted with my Business.*

If someone is in your social network, especially your small circle of friends, even when you really can't remember how you originally met him, you should be able to trust him with your business. Right? He's an investment banker and he got into selling XXXXX Miracle Juice from the Amazon. Well look how well he is doing? He has a Ferrari, a Jaguar and a house in the Hamptons. He knows what he is talking about. Or are those merely photos (of someone else's Ferrari, etc...) and did he tell you that he had that house in the Hamptons before he starting selling the XXXXX Miracle Juice from the Amazon? How about the fact that XXXXX is a MLM (Multi Level Marketing) business and he makes money on people he brings in and many, not all MLMs are scams.

Not to waste your time with every MLM scheme using social networks today, or other fraudsters using them, just go back to Chapter 4 and refresh your memory about what happened to MaryBeth, Jonathan and Sandra. Social networking as a business tool is exceedingly popular and almost as popular as a fraud tool for con artists and other criminals.

Social Network Lie Number 7: *We met on Facebook, you can Trust Me!*

Can you really trust a man you met on your social networking site? If your friends trust him to have access to their children's photos and most intimate conversations, then you can too! You think? **NOT!**

Good News

The good news is that you can use the information and investigative techniques in this book to investigate people you meet before you meet them, before you trust them with your friends, before you trust them with your money and before you trust them with your heart.

Chapter 17

Is your boyfriend, spouse or significant other sneaking around on YOU, online?

What about your significant other? Is he sneaking around on you, online? How can you tell? Are there any telltale signs? What are those signs? Well, here is what we call the 11 Red Flags of Online Cheaters. The more red flags you see, the more snooping you should do.

Too Much Online Activity

His online activity goes beyond what is the normal amount of time spent by most people. It may also involve suspicious or secretive online activity, such as late night web surfing, emailing, chatting and getting up at night to go online.

Protecting Financial Transactions

Whether he has done so in the past or just starting doing it, he is hiding some of his expenses. He may have suddenly started to pay the credit card bills on his own. Cash withdrawals have become more frequent. This may be to cover his tracks. Credit card statements, certain locations where cash withdrawals are made, and other transactions can provide great insight to the extracurricular activities of your man. Also, by protecting his financial transactions, he can be covering up Internet transactions he doesn't want you to see and stopping your ability to access online accounts or change passwords.

His Computer is Inaccessible to You and other Family Members

He's told you that he has important files on his computer and can't take the chance that someone, like you or the kids, may accidentally delete those files, therefore, he has put a password on the computer or has it locked up. This should be especially suspicious if you previously had access to the computer and it wasn't a problem. Is it because of his work or is he trying to keep secrets from you. Are these secrets something, or someone, you may be very angry about?

You See Dating Sites and other Suspicious Activity in his Search History, Browser and Email In-Box

When you work on the (his) computer, you notice in the Search History and Browser there are names and URLs of dating sites, florists and names of women you don't know. Maybe it's just innocent or maybe he's just looking for (and found) some action, other than you. And if you happen to see his Email In-Box and there are emails from Singles Websites and Online Dating Websites, he is more likely, than not, visiting these sites.

He Has Several Email Accounts

It is quite common for people to have more than one email account. Usually, there is one for work and one for personal use. But when someone has several personal email accounts, it leaves a lot of room for speculation or concern.

He is Accessing His Business Email Account from Home

What might have been the occasional, or even non-existent, access to his business emails has become a regular pastime. Frequently accessing his business account, especially when he makes more than one trip each night or works late online may be a signal that your significant other is doing more than just work at home.

Frequently Changes his Internet Service Provider

Is he trying to hide from someone or is really fickle about the best Internet service available. Maybe he just likes change. Like women change their shoes, men change their ISP...NOT! Men who frequently change their Internet Service Providers can be escaping the clutches or contact of someone, usually a female, he doesn't want to track him down anymore.

Abruptly Changes his Cell Phone Number

He tells you he has been getting prank phone calls and had to change his home phone number or cell phone number. Strange that you never heard about these prank phone calls before, but then again, he did get a lot of hang ups and wrong numbers. Well, at least that's what he has told you.

Leaves His Laptop at Work

He used to bring his laptop home all the time. In fact, he used to work in bed right next to you. Now, he leaves it at work and it has been going on for quite some time. Is there something on that laptop he doesn't want you to see? Or maybe he is afraid you might want to do some online surfing on his laptop like you used to and you'll see what's really going on.

Abrupt Computer Shut-downs When You Come In

Of course it could be a coincidence that he is shutting down the computer when you walk into the room and your suspicious mind is just playing into this cheating thing. However, if you happen to notice computer shut downs often when you walk into the room, maybe he is doing something on the computer he doesn't want you to see like that ring he has been researching for the past few months or that vacation he is going to take you on. Maybe it's just something he doesn't want you to see!

He Has His Own Social Networking Account(s)

Your joint or family Social Networking Account, like Facebook, apparently is no longer enough for him. He has opened up his own social networking account and he hasn't had a chance to invite you in as a friend. Maybe, he even tells you his new account is only for business clients, not friends. Maybe it is! What do you think? We think you need to investigate.

To uncover online cheating, try the following sure-fire SECRET investigative steps. CAUTION! In no way are we telling you to break the law. You have to use common sense when following these steps and use your own judgment on how far you are willing to go:

A.   First, do not confront him until you have your entire investigation complete. If you are not fully prepared, you will give him time to cover his tracks and his ass.

B.   Second, analyze all your information that you compiled up to this point. This will help you decide how and which way to focus your investigation and when. You will not want access accounts that will alert him. You will also not want to get caught doing it. Make sure he is not around when you start your investigation.

C.   Install a key logger on the computer that he uses so you can track his online activity. There are many ways to do this, which is a separate book in itself, and care must be taken when downloading software from an unknown source. We suggest reviewing websites that discuss parental monitoring of children (how appropriate!), and some of the suggested software manufacturers used to track online activity.

D.   Check the internet history. One of the most overlooked files on a computer is the internet history folder. If you, or he, use a Windows operating system, you can check the internet history to see what websites he has been visiting. Every time someone logs onto a computer and surfs the web, the computer keeps a 'cached' image of the websites in addition to any 'cookies' that were deposited during the visit. In layman terms, the computer takes a 'snapshot' of the website so it can refer to it faster next time. 'Cookies' are small files that store information about the computer's user, the visits, and some basic information about the sites visited. This is especially important because most secure online transactions, such as banking, finance, etc, typically require that the computer's browser accepts cookies as part of its use. If you know your man has a bank account with Wells Fargo bank, and you find cookies for several different banks, then there is something wrong. Either he is not disclosing something or he may be searching for a different bank altogether.

E.   Acquire the Passwords – If you have installed a key logger on someone's computer, there is a good chance that you have obtained a password or two based on their online activity. If that is the case, you probably will notice that most people reuse the same password repeatedly, regardless of the type of information that it is intended to protect. People often use the last four digits of their social security number, birthday, children's date of birth, military boot camp number, etc. Oftentimes, the same password is used for just about everything, from banking to e-mail to accessing a YouTube account. And once you have access to the password you have access to his life. If all else fails, just ask him for it. You would be surprised how many people divulge their passwords when asked.

F.   Identify the IP Address – In Chapter 21, we will discuss how to conduct a reverse lookup of an internet IP address in more detail. If you are at his house, and he has unsecured WIFI then all you have to do is connect to it. You can do it on your phone or laptop. It doesn't matter. Upon logging into his WIFI, conduct a Google search for "What is my IP address", and utilize one of the many sites to determine what the address is at his house. Once you do that, you can search the ARIN database to see who owns that IP address. Keep in mind that this IP address may appear in an unsuspecting e-mail to a lover or a friend, which you can trace back to him. Write it down, since it may be important later.

G.   Identify his Social Networks – If your friend has a social networking account, which he claims is for 'clients' only, maybe it is time that you become a client. Create a fake social networking account based on the type of business that he performs. If it is true what he says then you should have no problem becoming his friend. Once you're in, you can see what is really going on.

Chapter 18
What about <u>YOUR</u> reputation online?

Turn on the television, and you will read news report after news report about information posted online being used against someone in a criminal, civil, or even an employment setting. There have been numerous cases of law enforcement officers being fired because of comments they had made on Facebook or MySpace, and the photographs they posted on them. There is nothing we can do in this day and age to prevent our information from becoming public. The only thing you can do is search for derogatory information about yourself, and find ways to remove that information from the hosting website.

If you are just in the beginning stages of starting an online life then we suggest you STOP RIGHT NOW. The sure bet in protecting your online reputation is to NOT BE ONLINE, however, unless you live in a cave you will have no choice in becoming involved with the Internet. If you are a parent, teacher, employer, girlfriend, wife, lover, etc, you probably should be aware of what is going on online, and hopefully learn how to deal with whatever may be found. In this chapter, we will talk about the various ways you can protect your reputation online on your own, and we will discuss some of the fee-based services being offered.

Search, Search, and Search Again

Throughout this book, we have demonstrated to you the power of the Internet, and the tremendous amount of information available online. Whether formal or informal, the same information you were able to obtain is readily available to anyone else about you. The question is what they will find. Do you know what is online about you? How much information have you shared with the online world? We would suggest you run the same checks on yourself that you would conduct on a potential mate. Your first stop should always be a search of your name, and any information about you. As the largest search engine, Google should be your first stop on your searching mission. Run a check of your name on Google, and see what turns up.

Google has made tremendous strides in protecting user information, which has been the result of protests from various privacy groups about the power of Google in general, and the amount of information they collect on us. In response to this, Google has attempted to inform its users on its privacy policy, and has provided some neat tools to track what kind of information is posted online about you. When you become a member of Google+ or Gmail, you can setup your profile to alert you every time your name appears on Google. This feature is called a "Google Alert", and is available to registered users. Google

"Alert" forwards you an e-mail every time your name appears in a Google search, and even provides you the link to the article that has the information in it. Remember, this feature is only available to registered Google users.

In addition to advising you of information available in their database, most search engines also provide you with an option to request that a search result be removed from their database. Bing.com even provides you with a convenient video tutorial on how to remove unwanted search results from their index. The key here is to look for the Terms of Service Agreement, and the websites Privacy Policy. These two documents will typically explain to you, the user, on how to remove unwanted information, and advise you of the kinds of information they collect on their respective sites. Get to know the websites that have information about you and look up their policies online, either at their "About Us" tab, or at the general "Help" page.

Privacy Settings

The use of privacy settings on various websites is another 'reputation protection' issue that should always be discussed. According to an article titled, "Reputation Management and Social Media" published in May 2010 by the Pew Internet and American Life Project, approximately 71% of social media users between the ages 18-29 have begun limiting the amount of information they share online by using their privacy settings on their respective accounts. This statistic is not surprising considering that more and more people are being scrutinized for what they post online. In fact, employers have attempted on numerous occasions to ask potential applicants for their social media usernames and passwords (although it has been struck down in some states). In law enforcement, background investigators have now begun vetting potential police recruits by searching online for derogatory information, inappropriate photos, and other online information. Do you know how much information you are sharing online?

If you have a social media website or any other personal webpage, you should be familiar with the privacy settings for each account. For example, who can see your profile online? If you never checked your settings, your entire profile is viewable by the public. This means if you are on Facebook, we can view your profile and we can download your individual photographs from your account. Scary, huh! With a simple change of your privacy settings, you can stop this from happening. By limiting your public profile to reveal only information you want to reveal, you can protect yourself from 'cyber stalkers' or 'creepers'.

Profile Lockdown

Probably the most efficient way to protect your reputation is to lock down your entire profile. When we say lockdown, we mean blocking everything with the exception of your name from being revealed. It is important to understand that the amount of information you post online will dictate the amount of information that people will be able to find out about you. Therefore, it is imperative that you are cautious on the amount of information someone may be able to obtain about you online. There are instances where you cannot control what is being said about you, but when it comes to social networking, you have ultimate control over what YOU reveal about yourself. Well, unless someone else reveals it about you without your knowledge.

When locking down a profile, the first and most obvious start would be the profile picture. We cannot tell you how many times we have found individuals, or at least information about them, by the profile picture that was publicly displayed. For example, one of the authors of this book was conducting a fraud investigation in which the suspects were passing bad checks and using their real identification. On one such occasion, a local merchant called the police about two of the suspects of the crime and how they both fled on foot in separate directions. Eventually, the two suspects, males in this case, were caught a short distance from the scene of the crime, but they adamantly denied knowing each other, and denied being involved in the crime. An online search was conducted, which revealed that both suspects had social networking profiles on Facebook and MySpace respectively. Within the profile photos of one of the males, a remarkable discovery was made, which changed the course of this investigation.

Can you guess what the discovery was that changed the course of the investigation? One of the suspects posted a profile picture of both of them sitting on the sofa, together, throwing up gang signs. We printed the photograph and brought it to court where the victim identified both of them and they were both charged with the conspiracy. You cannot make this stuff up! The key here is that they chose to post the photo and we simply recovered it. The old adage that "a picture is worth a thousand words" is quite correct in this circumstance, and resulted in a thousand hours of jail time.

Your photo is not the only thing that someone can see online. Think about the amount of information you have posted about yourself in terms of employment status, school, likes and dislikes, and other personal information. As we have shown you above, if we know where you went to school we can obtain information about you, and use that to get access to even more information. Why would you voluntarily give that away? As with most social networking websites, most of these fields are 'optional', meaning you have the option not to put anything in there. We would suggest taking that option and omitting this information when necessary.

Finding friends and connecting with people from the past is probably the biggest reason why most people join social networking websites. It has never been simpler to find someone online than on a social networking site. If you want to connect to High School friends, you simply enter your graduation year. Ironically, this can coincide with your date of birth, and 'bam' you can see members of your graduating class. If you find your old 'BFF' from High School, you can then look at her friends to see if there is anyone else on there that you might know, and connect with them. And so on and so on, until your friend count is over 1000 individuals, and you can read everybody's updates about the soup they ate or rants about their subway ride. You know who you are.

If your social network in real life consisted of 1000 people then you are a lucky individual and we applaud your 'social butterfly' status. However, if you are like us you probably had a small circle of 'true' friends that you hung out with and an even smaller group of individuals that you have remained in touch with (by phone or in person). It astonishes us every time we look up profiles, and find individuals with several hundred friends or even a thousand friends. If you think about it, your profile information may be private to the public, but what about your friends, or their friends, or friend's friends? You should have just left your profile public because having a thousand friends opens you up to the same issues if you had simply clicked "let everyone in" in your Facebook privacy settings. Of course, there is no such setting. We are just being sarcastic. The point is, you should be selective about who you allow in and periodically delete those individuals who you no longer talk to.

Have you ever been "Facestalked"? Do you know what a 'creeper' is? These are names for individuals who virtually stalk people online by perusing profile pictures, demographic information and anything you post publicly online. The website, Urbandictionary.com, defines "Facestalk" as "To look at pictures, read profile information, and/or repeatedly check the status of an individual on Facebook." This person can range from a good friend to someone who you have never actually met." The scary thing is just about everybody does it, but most do not readily admit it. There are numerous articles out there about victims who have been scammed by someone they had met online. When you look at why this person was selected to be scammed, you can clearly see that they left themselves open for it by leaving their profile unsecured or otherwise open for all to see. Whether it is photos, blogs, or any personal anecdotes you make in your status, all of this is useful to a con artist or someone who wants to do you harm.

Public Records

Have you ever committed a crime? Pause a second, and do not answer this one aloud. We want to be frank with you. Everyone has had something happen to them in their past that they regret. Unfortunately, some mistakes are harder to forget, and even harder to erase. This is where public records come into play. Public records are just that, 'records that are available to the public.' That being said, most information that is publicly available on the World Wide Web is ironically posted by the public. Duh! We have already told you to conduct a full search of any information that is available about you on the Internet. That was step 1. Now, what do you do when you find something online? The answer is not simple and requires a lot of work. Depending on the source of the information, the process may be a simple phone call or can range to an all out threat of litigation against the hosting site. However, if your reputation is important to you and the information posted is a serious affront to it, then the work may be worth it in the end.

The first types of public records you probably should be concerned with are State criminal, civil, and traffic court dockets. As we have demonstrated in the earlier chapters, there is a tremendous amount of information available from the government simply by the click of a mouse. Since we have already covered how to conduct a search on a 'Web Docket' system, we will discuss how to go about removing unwanted information from these sites. Unfortunately, most criminal, civil, and traffic court dockets cannot be taken down simply because you do not like that they are there. In most cases, a record can be removed by court order by a judge or some other statutory loophole you can use. For example, in Pennsylvania a defendant can have a summary offense expunged from his record provided he or she has not committed another crime for a period of 5 years. The types of offenses that fall into the summons or citation category are disorderly conduct, public drunkenness, harassment, etc.

In order to remove the record from the 'public' website, you will have to know whether such a statute or criminal procedure exists. We will always refer you to the power of the 'Google' search for that answer. Check your own State's Rules of Criminal or Civil Procedure to see if there is such a thing available. For those of you that may be reading this, and are currently facing some kind of criminal charge, you might want to talk with an attorney and ascertain whether there are first time offender programs you may be eligible for, which allow you to have a criminal charge erased from your records. Again, the easiest way to remove public records from the Internet is not to have one to begin with. Obviously, there are some things under your control, and some things that are not under your control, but you get the picture. Where there is a will, there is a way.

The second type of public record that generates many problems for individuals is their credit report or credit rating. Have you ever received unsolicited offers in the mail from a bank such as the Hokey Pokey Bank (not a real bank, trust us) offering you their platinum card with an excellent balance transfer interest rate? Of course, you have because we have received it as well. Unless you live under a rock and have absolutely no credit, chances are you have received something similar or a tremendous amount of junk mail. How do they get your information? Your credit report of course.

Under the Fair Credit Reporting Act (FCRA), consumer credit agencies may legally provide your name, address and credit rating information to other organizations for firm offers of credit transactions initiated by you, the consumer, and insurance purposes. There are many reasons why your information is shared according to the FCRA, and we suggest you read section 604 of the FCRA to get a better understanding of what we are talking about. Why is this important to you? You're not applying for credit, you are attempting to find a date. At this point in the book, we hope that you can already see the broader picture that we are painting. The information from the credit report is often the source of many of the address listings you will find on web. How many past addresses did you find on your self-search? You probably found a few or maybe all of your past addresses. Much of the white page listings come from this type of information.

So what can you do? Review your credit report for accuracy, and OPT OUT! If you find a discrepancy in your report you should be contacting the consumer credit agency immediately and have that information corrected or deleted. You can challenge any information in your credit report and the consumer credit reporting agency must conduct an investigation into the alleged discrepancy. The key here is to make sure you are on sound footing when you challenge something, which is why we suggest reading the FCRA. Another aspect to checking your credit report, especially if you are in a relationship with Mr. Wrong, is ensuring that there are no lines of credit opened that you do not know about. The following story illustrates the tragedy that can occur when you don't do it:

Jill was an administrative assistant at a Fortune 500 company and made a decent salary. She drove a nice car, and lived alone in her $150K condominium. Jill met her boyfriend online through a reputable dating website. Things began great. They both shared common interests, and got along wonderfully. The relationship continued for several months when her lover had come down with some financial difficulty. Jill, being the person that she was, offered to help her male companion by opening a line of credit for him in the form of a VISA account, which they both co-signed.

The relationship continued steadily for some time until Jill discovered that the reason her male friend had financial issues was because he was paying child support for a child she never knew he had, and to a woman she never knew existed. Needless to say Jill was not happy, and she broke off the relationship with Mr. Liar Liar pants on fire. Jill moved on professionally, and continued to date. One day, Jill received a statement in the mail indicating that she had a delinquent account with a major credit card company, which if not paid would affect her credit rating. Jill had contacted the company explaining that she did not have an account with their company, but they confirmed all of her personal identifiers with her, and advised her that she may be a victim of identity theft. The company requested her to contact the police, and file an Identity Theft crime complaint report.

Jill complied with the request, and she was presented with an Identity Theft Packet from the Federal Trade Commission. The first step in the process was to obtain her most recent credit report. Jill obtained her credit report, and was shocked by what she saw. It turned out that Jill had three delinquent accounts (One being the co-signed account with Mr. Liar Liar), and two retail cards. Jill was now $15,000 in debt and had to begin the process of repairing her credit.

The preceding story illustrates why reviewing and correcting your credit is so important. When it comes to reputation defense, your credit status can be important. If you are applying for a national security position with the government, your credit worthiness will play a part on whether you are hired. Additionally, your judgment will be questioned under the guise of 'character and suitability'. Now, Jill has several remedies at her disposal that she can use to fix Mr. Liar Liar, which include civil action and, of course, criminal action if it can be proven that he opened the fraudulent accounts. It's up to Jill to determine how far she wants to go with it. The obvious lesson here is to be very leery of a potential mate being in financial distress and offering up, probably, one of the most important things in your life which is your credit.

We had mentioned "OPT OUT" earlier, which is the next step in protecting your credit and yourself from unwanted solicitations. Under section 604(E) of the FCRA, you may elect to have yourself excluded from any agency releasing your information to outside agencies. Now, why would you want that? Easy, you can stop some of the junk mail that you receive at your home and prevent potential stalkers from obtaining a credit card application in your name from your own mailbox. In order to remove your name from these lists, you can contact each company directly and ask them how to do it or you can use an online form that is recognized by the FTC.

There are several "OPT OUT" sites out there, but the only ones recognized by the FTC appear on their site. To "OPT OUT" of prescreened offers of credit for 5 years, you can go online to www.optoutprescreen.com and enter your information online. Additionally, you can "OPT OUT" of direct marketing lists from various companies by going to www.dmachoice.org and opting out of marketing products. Another great tool is the "DO NOT Registry", which is a Federal program that allows a consumer to be taken off telemarketing companies lists. By being on this list, it should be easy to figure out if the person you are talking to is a criminal or attempting to sell you something. Either way, your response should be the same, *"I am registered on the Do Not Call registry and I do not answer solicitations on my phone."* Usually this works, but sometimes they still try to sell you something. For more information, we suggest visiting the FTC website at www.FTC.gov.

Websites

You have done your homework and you notice there are several sites out there that list your personal information. What do you do? The first step in the process is to check the Frequently Asked Questions (FAQs) or Help section of the site. Review the terms of service (TOS) or legal disclaimers and see if they tell you how to remove unwanted information (Duh!). Work smarter, not harder is our motto. Oftentimes, you will see ways in which you can make a request to the website host by e-mail or through a web based form the site offers. Fill out the information, and ask them to remove the information. Many times you may have to give them a reason why you want the information removed. If you are a law enforcement officer or a government agent, you can simply tell them that, and they typically remove the information from the site.

If you are not a law enforcement officer or government agent (You are probably better off), then you have several options ahead of you. If you are currently in an abusive relationship or have been a victim of a crime, you can request they remove your information based on your status as a victim. Most websites will honor such a request if they are a reputable company. Another option would be to request that certain portions of the information be removed such as the phone number or the specific apartment, etc. Your final option requires that your falsify information, which we do not suggest unless you have good reason to. Several good authors out there have some very interesting methods that may be of interest to you such as J.J. Luna and Frank Ahearn. However, we will choose to keep you legitimate for our purposes here.

The Reputation Business

People are astonished everyday by the amount of information they find online about themselves and are even more amazed by the sheer cowardice of some of the people who openly post false things about them. Why not? The Internet is anonymous. You don't have to face the person who you are commenting about, and let's face it, who cares? Unfortunately, a lot of people care, and they range from employers, government agencies, business partners, friends, family, and professional organizations. Look up any professional organization out there and you will find a "Code of Ethics" or some sort of disclaimer, which implicitly states that its members must adhere to certain ethical principles and behavior or be banned from the organization. Imagine, several hundred dollars later, you are banned from your organization because of a Facebook photo. How about being fired because of one?

Ask several police officers who thought they were cool posing with firearms on their Facebook wall, which were in violation of their department policy, and went against everything they were taught as an officer. Some were severely reprimanded while some have been terminated. What is clear is that your reputation does matter, but also that the reputation of the organization you work for also matters. And it matters more than you probably think! In fact, most organizations have developed strict social media policies, which prohibit employees from posting lewd, lascivious, or inappropriate photos that would be a discredit to the organization.

Therefore, it should come as no surprise there were several enterprising individuals who saw the "forest from the trees", and created a business opportunity from the chaos we call the Internet. A simple Google search (did we tell you how much we like Google) reveals over 28 million search results for the term "Reputation Defense Online." It is clear that the impact of the Internet on personal lives, businesses, and public officials has prompted the need for a way to monitor your "third life", which is your digital one. There was a time when you only had to worry about what happened at work and at home, and that was it. Now, you have to contend with what happens in the digital realm as well. While you are sleeping, your online life can run rampant and when you wake up you can find yourself in hot water with the wife/girlfriend, the police, your employer, and anyone else with a stake in your reputation.

Several companies out there offer 'reputation defense' services and are good at what they do. Some are useless, and some offer things that no one can provide, which is a guarantee that your reputation will always be protected. Most of what we teach you in this book is similar to the services they offer. However, I am sure there are things they do provide you that we do not. The point is as with anything, you must weigh out the pros and cons and decide for yourself whether the services offered are worth the price. Review what they offer, and check off their services based on what you have learned here when the information is of value to you, personally. As with dates, you should also investigate any businesses or partnerships you might engage in. You would be surprised how these techniques not only apply to your personal life, but may carry over to your business life as well. Have you heard of due diligence?

Lather, Rinse, and Repeat

Information is fluid and always changing, which is why you want to stay on top of it as often as possible. As we suggested at the beginning of this chapter, you probably should setup several "Google Alerts" with your information so you can be informed each time your name or personal information appears in a search. Google offers this valuable tool to its subscribers, which is completely free. It is important to periodically check your information to ensure that what you had removed remains removed. Many of these websites automatically update information as it becomes available so it is quite possible what you deleted last month may return to the same site. Be vigilant with your information and continually monitor what is being said about you or your reputation.

Chapter 19

Safeguarding yourself online from start to finish

Throughout the book, we have talked about how to investigate someone on the Internet. Although, the purpose of the information we have

provided to you is to help you protect yourself from online predators, it is also intended to help you become more aware of the dangers of the Internet. How do you protect yourself from start to finish? Well if we were Neo-Luddites, we would tell you to throw away all of your electronics and communicate with people personally or with written notes. And we would also tell you to never date online and pay for everything in cash. Since that would not go over very well with most of America, then the obvious answer is to follow a few simple steps we will show you.

Prepare for surgery

Okay, the title is a bit misleading, but before you begin your journey into the world of the Internet and online dating, you should act like your preparing for surgery. What do surgeons do before they perform surgery? They wash their hands and put on sterile clothing. Now we are not suggesting you simply was wash your hands and get a new wardrobe, it is a metaphor for starting out clean. You want to start out with a new e-mail account, which is specifically designated for your online dating activities. When filling out the e-mail registration information, you may want to omit some information. Specifically, just about everything. Loverboy does not have to know your real name. We suggest using a nickname or a preferred (cough) name if you have one.

Remember, the purpose of this e-mail account is not to have your bill payments, credit alert, and other important information forwarded to this account. The purpose is to receive your online dating e-mail and the SPAM that comes with it! And trust us, there will be a lot! If necessary, you can dump it at a moment's notice without leaving a trace that you owned it. If loverboy becomes a jerk, you can get rid of the account and he has no way of tracking you.

Next, if you plan to talk with anyone you meet online, whether casually or otherwise, (don't worry, we won't judge you for talking like that), we suggest a prepaid phone. We know, the only people who use prepaid phones are drug dealers and terrorists, but they do make sense in certain situations. The phones are anonymous, and nowadays you can get one for $10. The use of prepaid phones is not necessarily a criminal technique since it is also used in counterintelligence and counterterrorism work as well. So consider yourself sort of a dating spy (Mr. Bean, Spykids or Jane Bond) with your prepaid phone in hand. The principle behind the prepaid phone is two-fold. First, you get a phone number that you can give out to whomever you want. There is no account information tied to you (unless you enter it online, which we do not suggest), and it would be difficult for someone to trace your activities. The second benefit to a prepaid phone is that you can throw it away if Mr. Right does turn out to be Mr. Wrong. For $10, you can buy another phone, and start over new.

We cannot tell you how many times victims have given their number to some jerk who ultimately becomes an even bigger jerk, and bombards their phone with threatening messages, voicemails, and even go as far as tracking them via GPS (Family locator applications, etc). Victims rarely follow the advice of the police, which is that they should change their phone numbers. Often, the saga continues until the jerk is arrested, or worse, he follows through on his threats. Is it really worth it? For $10, you can take that issue out of the equation by saying goodbye phone, and goodbye jerk. Actually out of spite, I would mail the guy the phone with a note stating, "Here you go! Since you like calling and texting it so much, I thought I would let you have it."

Keep your profile clean. Too many of these dating sites ask a bit more information that is necessary to meet someone online. One site claims to use a series of questions to establish your compatibility with someone else and sends you a list of people who are compatible with you based on your responses. We need not delve into the science of this methodology, but we can assure you that if one of the authors decided to go onto a dating site we would definitely come up as a compatible mate in most if not all the searches. We can assure you that neither of us is the sensitive type, but we can be for the right price. Get it? Be careful what you post online. Fill out what is necessary to get you the account.

Next, you have to decide on whether you are going to post a profile photo of yourself. That is a tough one especially on dating sites because, statistically, you are probably going to get more hits if you have a picture than if you do not. However, we do not seem to get many hits on our gorilla photo because people cannot seem to take a joke. If you decide to post a photo of yourself, try to post one of you at a location other than where you live or work. For example, one victim used a profile photo of herself standing in her bedroom with her high school diploma and outgoing mail in the background. Needless to say, it didn't take too long, nor much effort, to figure out where she lived. A simple zoom feature using standard photo software was able to reveal her name, school, and an address off a bill. Be careful is the point we are trying to make.

Speak in Code

Well, maybe not code per se, but do you have to reveal that this is the third online dating site you have attempted in the last three months? What we are suggesting is that you don't show your hand before you see the rest of the deck. When you talk to someone, you can share stories and anecdotes about your life that you want to share, but be cautious on the amount of information you provide. YOU DON'T KNOW THIS GUY! So why would you tell him where you live right away. Remember, we are in an information gathering phase at this point, and if this guy is a professional jerk then he is also in the information phase. You can share the necessary niceties such as your likes and dislikes, but walk, do not run, with the rest of your information.

CATCH him!

Remember our earlier acronym, C-A-T-C-H, and how it applies to the decision making process of whether you should be with this person or not? The same process can be useful at the outset of a relationship because it gives you a process to assess the information he may be providing you. You want to **capture** any information he provides, and **assess** it against what you know, find, or verify to be true. This is obviously done through the various tools you have learned throughout this book. The next step is to **test** the information you learn from your search techniques, and evaluate it against what you have received from your target. The **critique** phase of the process will assist you in this evaluation step. Finally, you must decide on whether you want to **hold** the subject responsible for his lies (if that's the case). Do you confront him? It depends on what you want out of the situation.

Ultimately, by sterilizing your entry into the game so to speak, you have prepared yourself to make any decision necessary. If you want to sever ties with whomever it is you were interested in, then dump your email and get rid of the phone. Simply put, he doesn't exist anymore if you say so. There would be no way for him to contact you and harass you unless you have failed to protect information that could be used against you later. The key here is to limit the amount of negative exposure you will have with an unwanted mate. Make sure you utilize all of the tools at your disposal and re-evaluate your situation every time new information presents itself. That is the key to protecting yourself from start to finish.

Chapter 20

P.R.O.T.E.C.T.I.O.N. Tips for Internet Users

Procrastinate – Don't just rush to answer the message in your inbox! Did you use the cursor trick we showed you in one of the previous chapters?

Review – Review the contact from the person on the other end. Ask yourself, "what is it about?" Consider, who initiated the contact? Is it in response to something you placed? An ad? A dating profile? Was it unsolicited?

Organize – Organize your own investigation and keep a record of what you received and what you find out hereafter.

Think – Think about what they want from you or what they want you to do? Think about how much they know about you already? Are you vulnerable? Did you provide too much information already? Did you answer the person? Did you join up? Did you already link to their site?

Evaluate - Use a search engine, to search his catch phrases, email addresses, etc. Did you find them on Google, Yahoo, or others?

Consistency Analysis - Analyze the info you have uncovered and see where it leads you. Is it consistent? Is it varied and inconsistent?

Travel across the 'net - Go to formal FREE sites – Spokeo, 411, Pipl. com.

Investigate further – Use more accurate and detailed sites like the ones that law enforcement rely upon such as the paid sites - Intellius, LexisNexis, criminal records, court documents, etc.

Only you can decide - What does your gut tell you? Is this person a con artist, a potentially violent criminal, or a sexual predator? If you can't really decide, listen to what we recommend in the next letter, N.

Neutralize the threat - Cut your losses! Protect yourself! Change your passwords! Cut all contact with that person. Notify your ISP, the dating site or the police, if your investigation reveals that there is fraud or danger afoot!

Chapter 21

Quick Guide for Investigating Online Dates BEFORE you meet them

Before you date him, investigate him. Here's how!

Let's start with what you know about him. Ok, first, let's try the direct approach. What is his name? What is his first name, last name and middle name. What is his age? What is his birth date? Where does he live? What is his screen name? What is his telephone number? If you met him through an online dating site, you'll want to do a search of the profile name he uses there. He probably created that profile name from an active or inactive email address. He also may have created it from something that is significant or important to him like a nickname or sports team. Now let's take all this information and start searching.

Step 1 – The Google Search

Your first step in any investigation should be the standard search engine search. You will be surprised how much information you can find by simply putting a guy's name into the search field. However, be forewarned that if the guy has a common name like "John Smith" a simple search will be useless unless you add some additional information. Remember our Boolean search techniques. If you search for "John Smith", who claims to be from the Bronx, NY, then your search would look like this:

'John Smith' and 'Bronx' and 'New York (or any variation, such as legitimate abbreviations or modern shortened versions).

Step 2 – Public Records

The information that you obtained so far should have included, at a minimum, a name and a date of birth. Now it is time to find out if your guy is a jerk, a criminal, squeaky clean, or none of the above.

You want to check court records and public court dockets that may be available in your state. A simple Google search for "ANY STATE" web dockets" or "PA Web Dockets" will reveal whether there are online records you can access from the comfort of your home. Remember that you also want to check civil records as well in case there is a 'baby momma' somewhere you don't know about. There is a good possibility that you will find plaintiff and defendant information, which you will also include into your searches. For example, let's say he does have a baby momma, but you don't mind that he has kids. Let's say you run baby momma's information and learn that she has a criminal history a mile long to include attempted murder. Well then, I would hope your decision would be as easy as ours would be, which is to run, and don't look back.

Step 3 - IP Addresses

Another public record search you can perform is a reverse lookup of an IP address. Let say someone claims they are at a specific location like Los Angeles, CA and they send you an e-mail. As we have repeated throughout the book, everything you do on the internet is traceable. Within said e-mail, you can check the header information (message source, etc), and identify the IP address of the sender, which should correspond to the Internet Service Provider they use, and should be geographically near where they claim they live. How you say? Yes, each company provides its users with a specific IP address to access the internet. Depending on the service provider, the range of IP addresses will be the same for the geographic region, unless it is a large company like Verizon, but there is a way to narrow it down.

For example, the RCN cable company provides cable services to the Lehigh Valley, PA, area, Boston, MA, D.C. Metro, New York City, Chicago, and Philadelphia, PA. If someone claims he are from any one of these cities then his IP address should be consistent with this fact. So, let's say that you received an e-mail message from someone who claims he is from Florida and through his conversations he are telling you how beautiful it is down there, etc. You check the header information of the e-mail he sent you (typically by finding the options, and viewing the source information), and the IP address of the e-mail source is 207.172.12.4. Now with this information, you want to check with the American Registry of Internet Numbers (ARIN.net), which is one of six regional organizations that assigns IP addresses to users in the . You should only be concerned with ARIN at this point because you are checking an American IP address. You hope.

You perform what is called a WHOIS search of the IP address. Go to WHOIS.com to do it. Upon doing so, you learn that the abovementioned IP address belongs to the RCN Corporation. A simple Google search of the RCN Corporation and its service areas and you will note that RCN only operates out of those already mentioned areas with none of them being in Florida. At this point, you have received your first investigative clue that this person may not be who he says he is or he is being dishonest for some other reason. The scary part is if you live in RCN's service area, this guy might know who you are, and may be attempting to lull you into something. At least now, you are aware that something is not right and you can delve deeper into the matter or cut yours ties altogether.

Step 4 – Paid Services

If you went ahead and purchased a paid subscription to one of the suggested sites then now is the time to run it. Especially if you find some questionable information that you may want to further explore. More sites will offer a criminal history for as little as $6, which is nothing for the information that you will receive. Many times, you will also get a possible social security number, which will be valuable when looking through court records or finding out if there is a marriage license out there.

Step 5 – Business Check

Let's refer back to our story about the loverboy who needed his victim to ship products for him while he was away in London. We find that a search for business ownership is necessary to verify whether such a company exists or if your target is an officer in the company. Typically, the first place you should look for business information is the Department of State of the respective State or territory he claims to reside in. You will want to look up the Uniform Commercial Code filings, incorporation status, or any filings with the government agency that governs commerce and business transactions. Look to see if there is a website for lover boy's company. Contact the company and ask to speak to your lover boy by his real name (or the name he gave you). If you get the response, "No one works here by that name", that is what we call a clue in the investigative world.

Step 6 – Professional Licensing

Let's say Cassanova is a doctor who practices family medicine, or even better, he's a Pediatrician. He must love kids. You would want to check with the State licensing board where he allegedly practices, unless he has told you that he used to practice medicine and he is now in business for himself. Regardless, there should be an inactive license on file, which shows that he was licensed in the state to practice medicine. Either way, check it out. The same can be said for attorneys and other professionals who are regulated by a government agency. Make sure you check the status of their license and verify that they are who they say they are.

Step 7 – The Social Search

Although the amount of information you will receive from the previous searches will be highly valuable, and credible. Social Networks provide you with some very valuable leads that you can later fact check against your legitimate sites. You can search social networking sites one of two ways. First, you can do the old fashion search engine search and add the term "Facebook" or "MySpace" or whatever site you suspect they are on. You can use social network specific search engines like www.icerocket.com or www.spokeo.com and run a check against their databases. Secondly, you can log into the social networking site you suspect that the person is using and run a search for him online. There is a good chance that you will find his profile. Now you are left with two possible outcomes: One, the profile is private and Two, it is publicly viewable. If you are faced with the latter then you are in good shape. If the profile is private then simply find a friend in common who is not. It is quite possible that there will be information shared between the friend and your target that may be valuable to your investigation. Think about it. The comments, pictures, and tagged locations can say a lot about a person. Pay particular attention to this type of information. Additionally, if a photograph presents itself, you might want to consider capturing it as a reference for later.

Step 8 – The Photo Search

As stated above, if you obtain a social networking photo from one of your searches it can later be used against other photographs you find. Perform a search in Google or another search engine for images only and see what comes up. Typically, you will find various photographs that may or may not be related, but every now and then you get lucky. If someone tagged your Casanova in a photo you might want to see what the relationship is and does the same person continually tag him in his, or her, photos? That is typically a sign that they have a close relationship, but how close is the question. Dig on!

Step 9 – CATCH and Decide

Again, not to repeat what we have already covered, but you should be evaluating what you have so far, and making a decision on what to do next. The CATCH acronym will help you, but do not get hung up on it. Ultimately, you have to live with your decision, not us.

Step – 10 Move on

We cannot emphasize this enough. Once you have made a decision to dump someone due to your investigation, MOVE ON! Past behavior is a good predictor of future behavior. Do not think that you can possibly change him, and it will not happen to you. The fact is the only thing you can control is yourself. We have seen this mistake repeatedly and sometimes the ending is okay, but most times, it is not. This is why we emphasize the investigative aspects so much. You are making an informed decision. Believe in yourself.

Chapter 22

What the police need from you if you are a crime victim and why you should have it.

We decided to include this chapter for many reasons, but mostly because we see women (and men) everyday who have become victims of Internet crime and there appears to be a lack of consistency with regard to the way these cases are handled by police officers throughout the country. There are departments who are prepared for Internet crimes and have dedicated fine men and women who are good at what they do. However, many departments lack knowledge, manpower and resources to handle these types of cases, which is a crime in itself and a disservice to the public. Although this may be the case, we felt it important to at least provide a list of things that you can do to assist the police and give them a head start on the investigative process, whether you are the victim or someone you know.

Whether the crime is cyber stalking, harassment, terroristic threats, black mail, etc…, the stories are always the same. Most of the victims believed at some point that the person on the other end cared for them and thought that they would change. Many entered into relationships believing that their instincts were wrong because of what their eyes were seeing. The first and foremost recommendation we can make is follow your gut. We are not too proud to admit that women have better instincts than men do, but women tend to doubt themselves a lot more. If you still doubt your instincts then let the contents of this book assist you in making a fully informed decision.

If you or a friend is a victim of an Internet related crime, we want you to follow these steps before you call the police. Not only are you assisting the police in their investigation, but you are also helping your own cause by ensuring that your case will be investigated. That is especially true when you have handed the investigator what he needs to prosecute Mr. Wrong.

Step 1 – Recognize that you are a Victim

The first step in any criminal incident is to recognize when you have become a victim of a crime. Whether it is harassing text messages, inappropriate wall postings, threatening e-mail, or black mail about posting nude photos of you (which in hindsight you probably should have never taken and given to him in the first place) you are a victim of a crime. The time to start collecting evidence is NOW!

Step 2 – Save, Save, Save

One of the worst things you can do is to delete threatening messages or comments you receive from your suspect. Whether he apologizes or not, you need to keep everything he sends you. If it is an e-mail, create a special folder in your e-mail box and label it "Jerk." Every time he sends you another message, you simply move it into this folder. If he posts something on your homepage, print it out and save it. Why? Because he can remove his own post, and deny every posting it.

Text messages are another problem. You can now send text messages from Yahoo!, Google and other e-mail providers without a phone. Recognize when someone is sending you text messages from one of these sites and save it. If you know he uses Yahoo! make sure you write that down. Save, Save, Save!

Step 3 – Respond with one sentence

If someone is continually harassing you, sending you messages, and calling you at inconvenient hours, do not call that person back! Send the person a text message or e-mail with the following statement:

"Dear_____, I have told you repeatedly that I do not wish to receive any more messages, phone calls and other correspondence from you. I am asking that you discontinue any and all communications to me or I will be left with no choice, but to report you to the local police. I feel harassed and I fear for my life."

Ensure you save this text or e-mail as proof that you have asked this individual to stop harassing you. The date and time of this text will be important.

Step 4 – Send to Voicemail

One of our favorite pieces of evidence is the voicemail message. There is nothing more potent in terms of evidence because you have the suspect's voice right there on tape. Many victims answer the phone and give the suspect the opportunity to spew his nonsense at them. Why go through all that? I suggest forwarding them to your voicemail each and every time they call you. Eventually, they get frustrated and give you exactly what you need, proof!

Step 5 – Gather suspect information

This is self-explanatory, but we will explain it anyway. What is his name, address, and phone number? How about his handle or screen name? Does he use a particular e-mail address? What kind of device does he use? Is it a cell phone, landline, laptop, desktop, or work computer? What is his level of computer literacy? Does he work at the Geek Squad? Is he a gangster with no computer skills? These are important questions that you should have answers to before you go to the police.

Step 6 – Bring your evidence

Before you go to the police, make sure you have everything you need get this investigation going. Bring the computer printout with the harassing messages. Don't show us a Facebook post on your cell phone. Print it out. Print out your phone bill in advance. If you have a prepaid phone then contact the phone company and find out if there is a log of calls that you have made and whether you can obtain it.

Step 7 - Write a Statement

During your investigation, you should have taken notes on each incident that has happened with Mr. Wrong. Be prepared to type out or handwrite a written statement reflecting everything that has happened and how you feel about it. It is important that you express how he has made you feel, emotionally and physically and what kind of danger you feel you are in. This goes a long way at ensuring that something is done. It is great evidence for a prosecutor to be motivated to aggressively prosecute the case and it is even better for a jury to hear. Since, you know his history because you looked him up, mention this in your statement. Always be truthful. Did you respond in anger? Did you send him threatening messages? Be up front about what you did as well. It is natural to respond with anger when you are angry and frightened.

Step 8 – Be Patient

Many people go to the police believing that they know how to do their job. Frankly, if a case could be resolved in 30 minutes like on television, there really should be no crime to write about. The fact is that the police are constrained (rightfully so) by the laws of our country and there is a tremendous amount of paperwork involved. The advantage you now have over the officer is that anything you do is not subject to the same laws, rules, and regulations that the officer is obliged to obey. For example, if you see that your boyfriend is viewing child pornography on his computer and take the computer from the house to give it to the police we can use it. However, if an officer goes into a house and takes a computer without probable cause then they just violated that person's civil rights. The evidence can be thrown out and he can sue the police. See the difference.

That is why we are giving you these steps to follow before you come to the police. In essence, you are not only helping your own case, but you are making it easier for the officer to do his job.

Step 9 – Be a good witness

Without you, the case cannot proceed forward, and the bad person will not be put away. The investigation does not end with the police arrest. There is a possibility that you will testify in court. As a victim of a crime, you have rights, and you have an obligation to the court. Remember to testify truthfully and do not omit anything. If you made a mistake, admit it. Keep in mind that you are not only testifying about your own case, but for the victims this guy may have already hurt or will hurt in the future.

Step 10 – Move on, and be cautious

If you were involved in a bad relationship and survived it, you are one of the lucky ones. There is an old saying, *"Those that do not know history are doomed to repeat it."* You should learn from your mistakes and move on. You now have the ability to protect yourself by ensuring that you will never be victimized again. That is our hope in creating this book.

Remember, to save trouble, BEFORE YOU DATE HIM, INVESTIGATE HIM!

Appendix A

Glossary of Terms, Definitions and Abbreviations

123 – ASAP; At Once; Immediately; Right Now

187 – Murder; Kill; California Penal Code for Murder

2NITE – Tonight

20 – What's your twenty?; 10-20; Address; What's your location?

211 – Robbery; California Penal Code for Robbery

411 - Information

420 – Marijuana friendly

50 – Five Oh; Police; Parents; Spouse

51 – One card short of a full deck

6 - Six code. It is used by school aged children (Middle School and older) as a typed/texted code to alert their friends that parents are entering the room and to refrain from sex, drugs and other forbidden behavior talk. 66 is used to mean the coast is clear and it's OK to talk that way.

7 – Lucky

77 – GG; Gotta Go!

86 – Get Rid of It; Eighty Six it!

8732 – USDA; American Made; Alphanumeric Telephone code for USDA

A – Asian

ADDY – Address

AFK – Away From Keyboard

AKA – Also Known As

AML – All My Love

AnyWHO.com – an online people search engine similar to your standard white pages.

AOL – America Online; One of the earliest Internet Service Providers that is still popular today.

App – Application; A software program.

ASAP – As Soon As Possible

AshleighMadison.com – A dating site for cheaters

AYLYAO – And You Laughed Your Ass Off

B – Black

B4 – Before

BBL – Be Back Later

BBW – Big Beautiful Woman

BDSM – Bondage, Discipline, Domination, Submission, Sadism, Masochism

BeBo – A social networking site

BF – Best Friends

BFD – Big Freakin Deal

BFF – Best Friends Forever

BHM – Big Handsome Man

BIF – Bi-Sexual Female

Big Church – A dating site where members are listed according to their religious preference.

BIM – Bi-Sexual Male

BIMF – Bi-Sexual Married Female

BIMM – Bi-Sexual Married Male

Bitmap – The term bitmap comes from the computer programming terminology, meaning just a map of bits, a spatially mapped array of bits. A type of image.

Bookmarks - Web site URL addresses saved on a browser to make returning to the site quick and easy.

Browser - The software that allows for viewing Web pages and searching the Internet (Think Internet Explorer, Firefox, etc...)

C – Christian

Catholic Match - Website devoted to Catholic singles.

Catholic Singles - Online dating site devoted to Catholics.

CD – Cross Dresser

Chat Room - An area on an on-line service of the Internet that allows real-time, typed-in communication with other people.

Chemistry.Com - Is billed as a sister or related site to Match.com because it was created by workers who were part of the other site. The site only allows registered members to see 5 matches a day unless they pay to register for the other features.

Christian Café - Online dating site for those with Christian beliefs.

Classmates.com – Also known as memorylane.com, this social network site offers members an opportunity to connect to former classmates by either connecting you with an already established profile or e-mail former classmates to become members.

Cookies - Text files that are placed on the computer's hard

CP – Sleepy

CPL – Couple

CU – See You

CUL8R – See You Later

CWYL – Chat with You Later

D – Drinker

D&S – Dominance and Submission

DateHookup.com - Free personals and free online dating.

DBF – Divorced Black Female

DBM – Divorced Black Male

DDF – Drug and Disease Free

Directory of Dating - http://www.directoryofdating.com/; An Internet dating directory that provides ratings and reviews of the most popular dating sites.

DBD – Death Before Dishonor; I'd kill myself before I'd embarrass myself or my family

DBS – Don't Be Stupid

Discussion Group - Also known as 'Newsgroup'. A group on Usenet devoted to a certain subject of common interest.

Dom – Dominant Male

Domain Name - The unique name that identifies an Internet site, separated by periods and following the type of protocol accepted: http://www or FTP, for example. Some common domain categories are: *.com (commercial); *.gov (government); *.mil (military); *.edu (educational); *.net (Internet service); *.org (non-profit organization).

Domme – Dominant Female

Download - To electronically copy a file from one computer to another computer.

DWF – Divorced White Female

DWM – Divorced White Male

Ebony – Black Female

eHarmony - is a paid dating site where members fill out personality profiles and they're matched in different categories and areas of their personality. The site has been the target of some controversy lately because they refuse to match gay and bisexual applicants.

Email - Electronic Mail

Email Address - The exact Internet address where email can be received and sent. It utilizes the @ sign prior to the domain name.

Emoticons - Typed characters in e-mail or news postings that, when viewed sideways, represent faces expressing an emotion, such as :-)

Ezilion Date - European based online dating site.

F – Female

F2F – Face to Face

F4F – Female for Female

F4M – Female for Male

Facebook – Facebook is a social networking website that was originally designed for college students, but is now open to anyone 13 years of age or older. Facebook users can create and customize their own profiles with photos, videos, and information about themselves. Friends can browse the profiles of other friends and write messages on their pages.

FAQ – Frequently Asked Questions

FAQ - Frequently Asked Questions.

Firewall - A combination of hardware and software that protects a LAN or single server from unauthorized access through the Internet.

Flame - An offensive on-line message or personal attack.

Flowmingle - is a unique site because it doesn't rely on testing or matching of members. Members join and setup their own profile page, similar to MySpace. They can then respond to questions, meet other members, and form their own matches.

Forum - An online area devoted to the discussion of a particular topic.

France Dating - online dating website for people living in France.

Friendster – An older social networking site with profiles, and friend lists similar to many popular sites

Friends with Benefits (FWB) – Sex without attachment

FWB – Friends with Benefits

FYI – For Your Information

G – Gay

GBF – Gay Black Female

GBM – Gay Black Male

Geo-tagging – The embedding of GPS information in the metadata of photographs identifying the location of where a photograph was taken

GIF - The Graphics Interchange Format is a bitmap image format that was introduced by CompuServe in 1987 and has since come into widespread usage on the World Wide Web due to its wide support and portability.

GMTA – Great Minds Think Alike

GRRR – Growling

GSOH – Good Sense of Humor

GTG – Got to Go

GTSY – Good to See You

GWF – Gay White Female

GWM – Gay White Male

H – Hispanic

HAGN – Have a Good Night

HD – Heavy Drinker

HH – Heil Hitler (White Supremacist beliefs)

Home Page - Refers to a World Wide Web screen available on the Internet. Also known as a Web Page

Hook Up – Met; Get together; Sex

HS – Heavy Smoker

HWP – Height/Weight Proportional

Hyperlink - Also called link. Connects the user on hyperlinked words or graphics to go to a new Web page

Hypertext - Underlined or different color text contained in a web page that allows the user to click on it to move to another web page or Internet link.

ICQ – I Seek You (Chat Software)

ILU – I Love You

ILY – I Love You

IM – Instant Message

IMHO – In My Honest Opinion

IMO – In My Opinion

Intellius – A fee based service that offers background investigation services, reverse phone and address lookups, and other investigative services

Internet - The worldwide matrix of connecting computers that started as a government defense project in the 1960's and has since become a mixture of government, educational and commercial networks.

Internet Relay Chat - Allows users to converse with others users by typing comments on their keyboards and reading responses on-screen in real time.

Intranet - An internal link, utilizing a LAN or WAN, that features the same type of interconnectivity and communications features as the Internet.

IP Address - Internet Protocol Address. All Internet connections have an IP address consisting of four sets of 0-255 numbers. The IP address is usually generated by the modem.

IRL – In Real Life

ISO – In Search Of

ISP - Internet Service Provider.

IT – Internet Technology or Information Technology

IWSN – I Want Sex Now

J – Jewish

JPEG - Joint Photographic Experts Group. A type of digital photograph.

K – Kiss

KOTC – Kiss on the Cheek

KOTL – Kiss on the Lips

L – Lesbian

LD – Light Drinker

LDR – Long Distance Relationship

LDS – Latter Day Saints

LexisNexis – A fee based data mining company, which is a popular law enforcement resource. Provide various information services to include public record searches, and background investigations

LFG – Looking for a Group

LHU – Let's Hook Up

Link - Short for "Hyperlink"

Listserv - A form of electronic subscription service relating to newsletters and other on-line publications featuring a particular topic, or from a particular source.

LMAO – Laughing My Ass Off

LMIP – Let's Meet in Person

Log On - To gain access to or sign in to a computer system.

LOL – Laugh Out Loud

LOLTM – Laughing Out Loud To Myself

LS – Light Smoker

LTR – Long Term Relationship

M – Male

M4F – Male for Female

M4M – Male for Male

M6 - Mix

M8 – Mate

M9 - Mine

MAC (address) – A MAC address is a hardware identification number that uniquely identifies each device on a network.

MAF – Married Asian Female

Match.com - is one of the largest dating sites in the world. Members receive matches from the company, but they can also search for users who match their specific requirements.

MBA – Married But Available

MBF – Married Black Female

MBL – Married But Looking

MBLFF – Married But Looking For Fun; Married But Looking For Friend(s)

MBM – Married Black Male

MCF – Married Christian Female

MCM – Married Christian Male

MHF – Married Hispanic Female

MHM – Married Hispanic Male

MJF – Married Jewish Female

MJM – Married Jewish Male

MM – Marriage Minded

MMF – Married Muslim Female

MMM – Married Muslim Male

MNC – Married No Children

Modem – Modem is short for *modulator - dem*ODULATOR. It is a device or program that enables a computer to transmit data over telephone or cable lines.

MWC – Married With Children

MWF – Married White Female

MWM – Married White Male

My LOL - A free dating site targeted towards teenagers.

NA – Not Applicable

NB – No Baggage (children, ex-spouses)

NBM – Never Been Married

ND – Non Drinker

Neo-Luddites – People who have a personal world view opposing many forms of modern technology. Its name is based on the historical legacy of the British Luddites, who were active between 1811 and 1816. Neo-Luddism includes the critical examination of the effects technology has on individuals and communities.

Net - The Internet.

Netiquette - Internet etiquette

Network - Two or more connected computers that communicate with one another

Newsgroup - Discussion groups that focus upon particular topics, comprising the Usenet.

NIFOC – Nude in Front of Computer

NS – Non Smoker

NSP – No Smokers Please

NSA – No Strings Attached

OK Cupid – A free dating site more popular with younger people under the age of 30.

OLDO – Online Dating Only (Does not want to meet in person)

OLL – Online Love

Online - The state of being connected to the Internet

Online Identity – Also referred to as someone's Online Persona, it is all the information available about a person online that he/she has listed. Some online identities may have inconsistent information.

OTP – On the Phone

P – Professional

Password - A private code used to safeguard access to restricted or limited use areas of computer systems.

PC – Personal Computer

PDF - Portable Document Format. A file format that reproduces word processing documents electronically, so they can be sent, viewed or printed exactly as they originally appeared.

People Search – It describes a type of search used to identify information on individuals to include name, address, and phone number

Perfect Match - paid site where members are matched with possible dates according to their answers on a compatibility and personality test.

Pipl.com – A popular white page people search directory

Plenty of Fish - a free dating site where users pick the type of relationship they want and search for matching members. They also have a separate forum for discussions on relationships, dating, and break-ups.

PM – Private Message

PNA – Pay No Attention

PO – Pissed Off

POFITS – Plenty Of Fish In The Sea

Posting - Sending a message to a Usenet newsgroup

POV – Point of View

Profile – A page containing personal information of a particular, which can include name, date of birth, and other pertinent information

PTD – Part Time Dater

PT – Part Time

QT – Cutie

Query – A search request

Real Christian Singles - the largest online dating website for Christian people.

RL – Real Life

RLF – Real Life Friend

ROFL – Rolling On Floor Laughing

RP – Role Playing

S – Single

Sep - Separated

S&M – Sadism/Masochism

SAF – Single Asian Female

SAM – Single Asian Male

SBF – Single Black Female

SBM – Single Black Male

SCF – Single Christian Female

SCM – Single Christian Male

Screen name – an online name or user identification that is unique to the individual

SD – Social Drinker

Search Engine - A tool that performs a text search on any word pattern or topic over the entire Internet. Google, Excite, Lycos, AltaVista, Infoseek, and Yahoo are all search engines. They index millions of sites on the Web, so that Web surfers like you and me can easily find Web sites with the information we want.

Shake My World - a dating website for those in Sweden.

Shareware - Software that can be downloaded from the Internet for free, but usually suggesting a small token payment to the author of the software.

SHF – Single Hispanic Female

SHM – Single Hispanic Male

SI – Similar Interests

SINK – Single Income No Kids

SJF – Single Jewish Female

SJM – Single Jewish Male

SMEM – Send Me an E-Mail

SMIM – Send Me an Instant Message

SO – Significant Other

Social Networking - Social networking allows its users to be part of a virtual community. These websites provide users with simple tools to create a custom profile with text and pictures. A typical profile includes basic information about the user, at least one photo, and possibly a blog or other comments published by the user. Advanced profiles may include videos, photo albums, online applications or custom layouts.

SOG – Single or Gay

SOH – Sense of Humor

Spam - Electronic equivalent of junk mail

Spamming - The act of sending multiple unwanted messages to a mailing list or newsgroup

Speed Date – A free dating site where members use pictures and webcams to go on speed dates and meet potential partners.

Spider - A spider is a software program that travels the Web, locating and indexing websites for search engines. All the major search engines, such as Google and Yahoo!, use spiders to build and update their indexes.

Spoofing – To spoof means to hoax, trick, or deceive. In the Information Technology world, spoofing refers tricking or deceiving computer systems or other computer users. This is typically done by hiding one's identity or faking the identity of another user on the Internet.

Spokeo.com – A popular search engine, which can search screen names, names, e-mail address, and associated social networking accounts

Spray Date - A Swedish oriented dating website that's broadening into other countries.

Sub – Submissive

Surfing - Navigating the Internet in a random browsing fashion

SWAK – Sealed with a Kiss

SWF – Single White Female

SWM – Single White Male

SYS – See You Soon

TD2M – Talk Dirty To Me

TDH – Tall, Dark, and Handsome

TG – Transgender

THNX – Thanks

THX – Thanks

TIAIL – Think I Am In Love

TIC – Tongue in Cheek

TIFF - Tagged Image File Format is a file format for storing images, popular among graphic artists, the publishing industry, and both amateur and professional photographers in general.

True - A paid dating site that runs background checks on members and blocks those who are married and those convicted of felonies.

TS – Transsexual

TV – Transvestite

Twitter – An online social networking service and microblogging service that enables its users to send and read text-based messages of up to 140 characters, known as tweets.

UK Dating – A subsidiary of Match.com intended for those living in the UK.

Upload - To send a copy of a file from one computer to another

URL - Uniform Resource Locator. This is the address that represents a web server and, as such, a web site.

UseNet - A worldwide network of Newsgroups

Username - The name of a particular user on a host, or server computer

VF – Very Funny

VN – Very Nice

Virus - A small computer program that copies itself over and over, usually causing some disruption or damage to the infected computer system. Viruses can be transmitted over computer networks.

W/O – Without

WE – Well Endowed

Web Page - A single document on the Internet as displayed by a browser

Web Site - A particular "place," or set of related pages, on the Internet

Webmaster - The operator or manager of a particular Web site

WLTM – Would Like To Meet

World Wide Web (www) - A graphical Internet system of communication that allows for the connection of millions of computers to thousands of servers worldwide

WT – What The?

WTF – What The F- - -!

WTR – Willing To Relocate

WUF – Where are You From?

WYCM – Will You Call Me?

WYRN – What's Your Real Name?

Xanga – a social networking site

XOXO – Hugs & Kisses

XRV – X-Ray Vision

YAHOO – You Always Have Other Options

Yahoo! Personals - began as a free site, but later went to a paid only service. Users can setup their own profile complete with pictures and search for those who match their criteria or let the site send matches.

YO – Years Old

YouTube – A video based social networking site, which is now owned by Google.com

YYSSW – Yeah, Yeah, Sure, Sure, Whatever!

ZabaSEARCH.com – A popular people search engine

Appendix B

Informational Sites

CYBER-STALKING RESOURCES

Crime Library – Cyber Stalking http://www.trutv.com/library/crime/
blog/tag/cyberstalking/index.html
A great resource for criminal cases involving cyber stalking, and cyber crime. Many of the stories provide insight into some of the strategies used by cyber criminals to entice victims.

Cyber Angels - Cyber Stalking
http://www.cyberangels.org/
A non-profit organization created by the famous Guardian Angels, which provides information on protecting yourself online. The site also provides guidance for parents, children, and offers cyber security tips.

Cyber Rights – Cyber Stalking
http://www.cyber-rights.org/
A website containing scholarly articles on cyber rights, and civil liberty protection on the internet.

Cyber Stalking – Cotse.net
http://www.cotse.net/
A website providing various internet related services to consumers directed towards privacy. The site has excellent resources on internet privacy, and internet security.

Cyberstalking – Halt Abuse
http://www.haltabuse.org/resources/stats/index.shtml
Website dedicated to halting online abuse. The website provides a wealth of information on protecting yourself online.

Internet Stalking – Revenge Site http://www.angelfire.com/ga/random/internetstalking.html
A private website that discusses internet stalking and revenge sites. The website provides personal stories of internet crime, and cyber stalking cases.

Get Netwise - Report Cyber Stalking
http://privacy.getnetwise.org/action/stalking/
A website dedicated to cyber investigations and educational references for parents and children.

Women Studies – Cyber Stalking http://womensstudies.homestead.com/cyber.html
A feminist website dedicated to women and girls. A page dedicated to providing information to victims of online stalking, and harassment.

IDENTITY THEFT RESOURCES

Federal Trade Commission Identity Theft Site http://www.ftc.gov/bcp/edu/microsites/idtheft/
This website is a one-stop national resource to learn about the crime of identity theft. It provides detailed information to help you deter, detect, and defend against identity theft. On this site, consumers can learn how to avoid identity theft – and learn what to do if their identity is stolen. Businesses can learn how to help their customers deal with identity theft, as well as how to prevent problems in the first place. Law enforcement can get resources and learn how to help victims of identity theft.

Identity Theft Resource Center
http://www.idtheftcenter.org
ITRC provides victim assistance at no charge to consumers throughout the United States. It also educates consumers, corporations, government agencies and other organizations on best practices for fraud and identity theft detection, reduction and mitigation. It provides enterprise consulting and outsourced services related to information breach, fraud and identity theft. Toll Free, No Cost Victim assistance is available from the ITRC at (888) 400-5530

President's Task Force on Identity Theft
http://www.IDTheft.gov
The President's Task Force on Identity Theft was established by Executive Order 13402 on May 10, 2006, launching a new era in the fight

against identity theft. Recognizing the heavy financial and emotional toll that identity theft exacts from its victims, and the severe burden it places on the economy, President Bush called for a coordinated approach among government agencies to combat this crime.

FRAUDS AND SCAMS

Craigslist Information about Scams
http://www.craigslist.org/about/scams
Craigslist provides information to help its website users, and the general public, identify scams and frauds that may be perpetrated by criminal users of their website. It offers awareness, prevention tips and resources.

Male Scammers
http://www.male-scammers.com/
Male-Scammers.com offers a vast array of useful tools to help report, identify and fight back against online male scammers. If you've been scammed in the past or you are suspicious that the male you are corresponding with may be anything but who he says he is, then you'll find information and tools to fight back.

Scams and Frauds at USA.gov http://www.usa.gov/topics/consumer/scams-fraud.shtml
This website provides tips to help avoid scams and fraud, as well as how to report consumer frauds and scams. Information is available on frauds and scams, including Banking and ATM Frauds, Credit Card Scams, Education Scams, Insurance Frauds, Internet Fraud, Phone Scams, Phone Billing Fraud, Cramming and Slamming, Benefits and Grants Scams, Business Scams, Cars Scams, Citizenship and Immigration Scams, Computers and Internet Scams, Family, Home, and Community Scams, Health and Nutrition Scams, International Relations Scams, Jobs and Education Scams, Money Scams and Travel and Vacation Scams.

Stop Scammers
http://www.stop-scammers.com
Stop-Scammers.com is a website that provides recent information on female scammers across the globe. They maintain an extensive database that lists known scammers together with corroborating evidence like correspondence, photos, countries of known operation

and documentation commonly used by such international thieves. If you've been scammed in the past or you are suspicious that the lady you are corresponding with may be anything but who she says she is, then you'll find information and tools to fight back. Stop-Scammers. com offers a vast array of useful tools to help identify and fight back against online female scammers.

Appendix C

Search Resources

411 Locate
http://www.411locate.com/
People, phone numbers, reverse look-up, data bases, etc.

Spokeo.com
http://www.spokeo.com
(People Search)

Ancestry.com (wide range of databases) http://www.ancestry.com/main1.htm

At Hand
http://www.athand.com/
A comprehensive, integrated Yellow Pages look-up

AT&T AnyWho
http://www.anywho.com/
Blackbook Online
http://www.crimetime.com/online.htm
Free data base searches

E-bay Search for Seller/Bidder Email Address http://pages.ebay.com/search/items/search-old.html
ICQ - "I Seek You"
http://homepage.icq.com/hp/
A Comprehensive Search Portal

NameBase – Public Records Research
http://www.namebase.org/

Public Record Finder
http://www.publicrecordfinder.com/

Public Records Searches – Search System
http://www.searchsystems.net/

Public Records Search and Real Estate – NETR Online **http://www. netronline.com/**

SearchBug
http://www.searchbug.com/all.aspx
Comprehensive, easily accessible directories for all types of searches

Urbandictionary.com (Internet Terminology Lookup) **http:www. urbandictionary.com**

Verizon National Super Search (people, addresses, phone) **http:// directory.superpages.com/people.jsp**

Zabasearch.com (People Search)
http://www.zabasearch.com

Bibliography

1. Pew Internet and American Life Project, Online Dating, Retrieved on March 22, 2012, from http://www.pewinternet. org/Reports/2006/Online-Dating/01-Summary-of-Findings/ Summary-of-Findings.aspx

2. Pew Internet and American Life Project, Online Dating, Retrieved on March 22, 2012, from http://www.pewinternet. org/Reports/2006/Online-Dating/01-Summary-of-Findings/ Summary-of-Findings.aspx

3. Marketresearch.com , US Dating Services Market, Retrieved on March 22, 2012, from http://www.marketresearch.com/ product/print/default.asp?productid=6773764#

4. The Victim Information and Notification Everyday (VINE) System, the National Notification System, Retrieved on March 24, 2012, from https://www.vinelink.com/vinelink/initMap. do

5. Icanstalku.com – about us, retrieved on April 24, 2012, from URL http://icanstalku.com/about.php

6. "Inside Google: The most powerful and successful technology company in the world"

7. "Family Portrait Turns Up on a Czech billboard" – Buzzfeed. com, retrieved on April 23, 2012, from www.buzzfeed.com, courtesy of KY3.com

8. Hock, Randolph, Extreme Searchers Internet Handbook: A guide for serious searches, Chapter 9, Addresses and Phones Numbers, Pages 166-167

9. About Us, Zabasearch.com, retrieved on April 8, 2012, from http://www.zabasearch.com/about_us.php

10. Nearly one-half of U.S. adults use some form of social networking site, along with hundreds of millions of people throughout the world [source: Russell]. These sites help people stay in touch with old friends or forge new connections, but they also present some serious threats. Much has been written about the loss of privacy or productivity caused by these sites, but one of the most common problems associated with social networking is often overlooked. Horror stories about child predators and romance gone wrong tend to grab the public's attention. For the majority of users, the problem may not be as extreme, but still lies in social networking users taking advantage of the medium's anonymity to stretch the truth.

11. Study after study illustrate that people are much more likely to lie online than they would in real life. In a 2010 report from Rutgers Business School, researchers found that people lied much more readily when using e-mail than they did when using traditional pen and paper. Participants felt they could get away with online lies because they believed that e-mail was less personal and not as permanent as the written word [source: The Telegraph 2]. In fact, online writings are the most permanent of all. Paper is easy to destroy, and may get lost or damaged over time, but the digital word is forever (at least in theory)

12. In a 2010 survey by Direct Line Insurance, just 20 percent of respondents claimed that they were more honest on social networking sites, while about 33 percent said they were more honest when engaged in face-to-face communication. Researchers believe this can be attributed to the lack of immediate consequences when one lies on the Web, versus dealing with the other person's potential reaction if caught lying in person [source: The Telegraph]

13. Surprisingly, members of online dating networks don't do a lot of lying. According to a study at the University of Kansas, people

involved in online dating networks keep lying to a minimum because they believe they will eventually meet dates in person, and their lies could be exposed [source: Jess]. In general, men on these sites lie more than women, except when it comes to weight. Men are also twice as likely as women to avoid face-to-face meetings to keep their lies from being exposed [source: Meanley].

14. In 2011, the BBC reported that one-half of British children between the ages of 9 and 12 have a Facebook account [source: BBC]. Given that Facebook maintains an age limit policy of 13 years and over, this indicates that a large portion of kids lie about their ages to set up profiles. Another U.K. study found that one of every two kids under age 18 lies online. Six of every 10 youth lie about their ages, and four out of 10 lie about their relationship statuses [source: Rasmussen]. These lies may seem harmless to kids, but parents should keep in mind the effects the lies may have on potential predators, and monitor children's online time accordingly.
    http://curiosity.discovery.com/user/bambi-turner/answers/page/3

15. Madden, M., Smith, A., "Reputation Management and Social Media", The Pew Internet and American Life Project, Pew Research Center, retrieved on April 25, 2012, from http://www.pewinternet.org/Reports/2010/Reputation-Management.aspx

16. Investigations Guild to Sources of Information, April 1997, US Government Accounting Office (GAO), Office of Special Investigations Publication

17. NIJ Special Report: Electronic Crime Scene Investigations: A Guide for First Responders; Second Edition

18. Shaw, Maura, Mastering Online Research: A comprehensive guide to effective and efficient search strategies, F&W Publication, Cincinnati, Ohio

18811175R00103

Made in the USA
Charleston, SC
22 April 2013